D.J. DIXON

Saint Jerk

D1518293

This novel is entirely a work of fiction. The names, characters and incidents portrayed in it are the work of the author's imagination. Any resemblance to actual persons, living or dead, events or localities is entirely coincidental.

Cover art designed in part using images from Dreamstime.com and Freepik.com

First edition

This book was professionally typeset on Reedsy. Find out more at reedsy.com

Contents

1

Let's Get Ready to Grumble

I think the word I'm searching for is *dread.* It wouldn't be quite right to describe my emotion as *fear*, which to me is when you worry about something that *could* happen but isn't certain. You *fear* that the free throw you're about to shoot will be an airball, or that the noise outside your window at night is a raging psychopath, or that you'll look like an idiot giving a presentation in front of your class.

Dread is worse. Something painful is definitely coming, and there's no way to avoid it.

A good example is the way I felt when my mom took me shopping for clothes before the start of this school year. Here I was about to begin eighth grade, my last year at St. Mary's when I'm finally the boss of the school, and my mom still insisted on going with me to clothing stores because she didn't want to risk the hassle of returning stuff online if something didn't fit right. At least she could have given me her credit card and let me do it myself. But no - once again, I had to endure the dread of facing that annual ritual of humiliation, and this year's was the worst.

I really didn't need more than a couple pairs of pants, having grown a little taller over the summer. Our school has a dress code, so my options were limited anyway, meaning it wouldn't take very long to find what I needed. We walked into the department store as we did every year, me and my mommy, on one of those mornings in late August when in spite of perfect weather, the sun seems to shine a little less magnificently with the realization that summer vacation is rapidly approaching its end. We sped past aisles of school supplies that would likely be replaced with Halloween costumes just a week later, and headed to the boys' clothing section in the back corner where the anguish would begin.

Mom promised it'd be over with quickly. Just find a style of pants in the right size, get one pair each in dark blue and gray, and we'd be on our way. Couldn't be easier, and Mom's work schedule was in my favor. She had to drop me off back at home so she could get to her shift at the clinic where she worked part-time as a nurse.

I suppose what happened next was my fault in some small way, but one rack of pants called out to me. Unlike the usual styles of boring pants that I and my classmates normally wore, these had cargo pockets all over and some neat stitching that would make me the envy of all the boys, and the dream of all the girls. I imagined myself keeping a variety of gadgets in my pockets, although none of it would be allowed by school rules. And since I wasn't yet an international spy, I didn't mind letting that daydream die. Still, they looked super cool.

Without turning to notice the disapproving look on my mom's face that I'm sure was there, I was quick to point out that the dress code only mentioned color.

"Okay," she said. "Find ones that fit and let's go."

Yes, let's do this and let's go. Because strolling over into the clothing section came two girls my age whom I recognized but didn't really know. They went to the public school, but in a town of about 30,000 people, you grow up seeing the same faces around the neighborhood. One of them was named Melanie, who was on a city league soccer team with me one summer when we were about 8 years old. Whether she also remembered that or not, we would never embarrass ourselves by actually saying hello or acknowledging each other's existence. It was like the opposite of a staring contest, where the first one to *make* eye contact is the loser.

I filed through the rack to find my waist size, but the closest thing they had was two inches smaller. Close enough. Meanwhile, Mom had located the same ordinary type I'd always worn before.

With my head down, I rushed into the changing room and tried them on. They were a little tight, but that was a price worth paying to look as good as I would. Besides, they'd stretch out the more I wore them. Now the challenge was to convince my mom.

I confidently peeked out to where she was waiting, hoping her eagerness to get to work on time would be my ally. I kept my distance from her analyzing eyes, clenched my rear cheeks together to make the pants fit as loosely as possible, and took two steps out from the changing room without making it too obvious that I was struggling to even bend my knees.

"Yep, these are good," I said quickly. "I'll change back and grab a gray pair too, then we can go."

The two girls had moved closer, looking through racks of athletic wear nearby. I don't know if they bought boys' clothes for themselves or were shopping for a boyfriend, but if the real reason they were hanging about was to see some entertainment, my mom was only too happy to deliver.

"Turn around," she said.

"They're fine."

"Just turn around," she insisted.

I pivoted around a few steps, trying not to lumber like a zombie as I clenched my buns so tight I thought I'd crush my pelvic bones.

"Jack, those are way too small. Come on. Let's get these," she said, two pairs of lame pants in her hands.

"Mom," I pleaded in panicked whisper. "They're fine. Can we just get these and go?"

Now I cared less about the pants than about getting out of this situation without further embarrassment in front of these girls.

"Jack, for crying out loud, those things are so far up your butt you'll need a tool to pry them back out!"

And thus was my dread transformed into shame. To the sound of the girls' muffled laughter, muted by jamming their faces in their purses to keep from waking the dead, I headed back to the changing room while Mom waited with the boring pants.

The one silver lining was that these girls didn't go to my school. Sure, they might tell their friends the story about some nameless kid whose mom made him look stupid, but no one would know who they were talking about, and I wouldn't have to face a thousand jokes from my classmates.

Although if they *had* gone to my school, maybe I could have gotten a cool nickname out of it, like "Steel Buns" or "Crowbar." The reality, though, is that none of my friends were clever enough to think of something like that. The unofficial giver of nicknames at my school was Tyler, and like in every other eighth grade on the face of the earth, he was top dog only because he was always the tallest and toughest, and even though he's sort of a friend, I have to admit he's not that bright. The best nickname he'd have come up with would be something like "Butt Pants" and think it was hilarious, and all the other guys would pretend it was too.

Fear can at least be a little exciting, in its own weird way, but dread is never fun.

And as I started the school year, a big plate of dread was on the menu. Because every year, the new eighth-grade class had to complete The Project - twenty hours of volunteering your own time in the service of others. Twenty hours of work that had to be finished by the end of the fall semester. Twenty hours that could have otherwise been spent on video games or naps.

The "Saints in Service" project was a tradition at St. Mary's. It was required as part of religion class for eighth graders for at least as long as I was a student there. Even when I was little, if I ever saw a kid from that year's class raking leaves or shoveling snow at a house I knew wasn't his, it would be a pretty good guess that he was doing it do earn hours for the Saints project, as everyone called it for short.

The whole purpose of the project was to send the class out into the community to do good things for others. And look, I understood why that's important, and so did my classmates, even if we would never admit it out loud while complaining about the project to each other. It's just that twenty hours is an awfully long time, and there would be no way to work that many hours without having to do some tasks that are a lot less fun than other things I've volunteered for in the past. Not only that, but you had to fill your hours by doing at least three different activities, none of which could be your own household chores.

Those rules meant I wouldn't be able to just wipe the dishes at home for a month and call it "service" when it was something I had to do anyway.

So I understood 'love your neighbor' and 'do unto others as you would have them do unto you', and all the other teachings that tell you to care less about yourself than about helping people in need. You don't even need to spend all those years at a place like St. Mary's to learn that, but it doesn't hurt, especially if you've got parents like mine and you grow up getting used to doing volunteer stuff once in a while.

But it feels different when it's something you have to do for school. I think if a got a homework assignment to watch football on TV, I'd whine that I'd rather read a history book. And twenty hours would be just so dang long. So when the school year started on a bright day in early September, the Saints project was at the top of the agenda for the year's first meeting of the Council of Surly Adolescents, also known as my lunch table in the cafeteria.

Of course, we didn't call ourselves that, but it was a pretty good description on most days. I don't know if every group of 13-year-old boys is like ours, but every conversation seemed to be a competition to show whose life was filled with the most terrible burden.

There were only twelve of us boys in eighth grade, and we had been pretty much the same group for nine years, counting kindergarten. Once in a while we'd have a new kid, or someone would move out of town or switch to the public school, but there were no changes since last year. Even the unwritten seating chart stayed the same. That meant nine of us sat at one long table, four along each side with one having to pull a chair to the end. Unlike some corporation, the kid at the end of our table wasn't the chairman of the board. No, our chairman was Tyler, and he always sat toward the middle where he oversaw the discussion, even if he rarely said much.

The other three boys in our class sat nearby at a round table. Year after year, it was always the same. In fact, that was our nickname for them – the Roundies, and as might be imagined, it was indeed Tyler who came up with that inspired bit of brilliance several years earlier.

Mike, James, and Walt always ate lunch together at that table, and then they'd usually keep to themselves during the outdoor recess before classes started again in the afternoon. That's just the way it was. It's not that they lived in a completely separate world from the rest of us. James had played on our school basketball team since fifth grade, and all three of them would join the rest of us once in a while during recess if we were doing something that interested them. Naturally, we all mixed in together in the classroom and on school projects. But they were never truly part of our core group of nine. Sleepovers, birthday parties (back in the days when we actually had those), or just hanging out after school - there was us, and there was them.

The funny thing was that we all got along just fine. They weren't unusually weird booger eaters, and they weren't super uber nerds. They were decent guys, and we treated them mostly well. The bigger idiots among my group might tease or push one of them around just to look good to Tyler or to show off to the girls. I have to admit to doing that a couple of times over the years, until I learned that the girls were less than impressed by that. Those three never did anything to deserve it, but they were an easy target for those of us trying to prove ourselves. Still it was never a huge injustice. The real butt-kickings always

7

took place among our closer friends.

And in thinking about it, maybe that's the reason they kept to themselves. The thing about the nine of us was that we could be rotten to each other. One accidental elbow during a playground basketball game could mean a short fight, then a few days of being an outcast to the rest of the group, depending on who hit whom. It wasn't written on paper anywhere, but Tyler was at the top of the list, with Mason right behind. Touch either of them, and if they were in a bad mood, you were on the outs with everyone for a while. The rest of us were constantly battling each other for any sort of status, and the deciding factors were athletic ability or your proclivity for annoying a teacher. I can't count how many sprints I've run against even my best friend Nate to decide who was faster. And I had an unspoken rivalry with Hector to be the smartest boy in the class.

Still, my classmates were the closest thing I had to brothers. Maybe closer, since we spent every school day together for almost as long as any of us could remember. And brothers fight a lot too, from what I understand. I wouldn't know, just having two younger sisters.

So while the Roundies gleefully did their thing, the Council of Surly Adolescents was called to order.

"What are you guys gonna do for project hours?" I asked as I plopped down in a chair and pulled a bologna sandwich from my paper bag.

"I'll volunteer to watch you do my homework all year," said Peyton, with a smirk on his face that was as stupid as his reply. Peyton considered himself the class clown, which tells you something about the level of comedic talent among my friends. He didn't get the laughs he was expecting, although of course if Tyler had said it, we'd all be fake-laughing our way onto the floor.

Ignoring Peyton, Mason chimed in. "I'll just make some stuff up on my report and forge my dad's signature," he said, and as proud as he was about this bad-boy declaration, we all knew he was full of it. Mason had a little bit of an edge to him second only to Tyler, but if he followed through on every one of his claims of misbehavior, he'd have been thrown in jail sometime around third grade.

"It's really no big deal," added Hector, bored as always by the rest of us. "You sign up for a few things on Ms. Garcia's list, and if you haven't hit twenty hours before Christmas break, just shovel snow for your neighbors or something."

Good grades came easy to Hector and me. The difference is that he didn't mind working for them when he had to, and that gave him the edge on being the teachers' favorite, which sort of irritated me.

The list he mentioned was a menu of options that Ms. Garcia, our religion teacher, put together to make it easier for us to find opportunities for service projects. It wasn't meant to get each of us all the way to twenty hours, but it was helpful not having to come up with ideas entirely on our own. For instance, she worked with the custodian to put together a schedule where we could sign up for one week of cleaning the classrooms for an hour after school. Nate and I signed up together for our week early in the year. From what I could tell, the custodian just walks through the main hallway and through each classroom with one of those wide janitor brooms. I could jog through that in about ten minutes and still count it as a full hour. Easy stuff.

Still, that would leave me with a lot of service time to fill. As the lunchtime conversation – if you could call it that – moved on to more important topics like which superhero would

9

be easiest to fight, I wondered why I was more anxious than everyone else about getting something like the Saints project done as soon as possible so I could forget about it. So now that I was a teenager, I figured I'd do what anyone else my age would, and decided that it was somehow the fault of my parents for raising me that way.

2

Service Error

I have a distinct memory of the first time my dad told me that everything on TV and in the movies is a lie. Actually, I can't be sure it was the first time, since I'm sure he said the same sort of thing while burping my infant self as he watched the screen, but once we were watching a show with a car chase scene that ended with a crash that caused a massive explosion and a fireball fifty feet high. My dad just laughed. "Why is it that every car on TV has a gas tank made of peanut brittle that holds a thousand gallons of jet fuel?"

Dad had taken it upon himself to supplement my education with a long lecture series over the years, with no apparent end in sight. In fact, these talks became more frequent over the previous few months as he dealt with the fact that I was entering my last year of Catholic school. I'd then be going to the public high school and, to hear my dad say it, there'd be a culture shock that he wanted me to be prepared for. It's not that he thought those kids were any worse than the dipsticks I went to school with; he himself went to a public high school. But he was concerned about keeping me grounded in the faith even though he believed that meeting more people with different backgrounds and viewpoints was a good and healthy thing for me.

As often as not, his speeches wouldn't have anything to do with religion, but instead related just to the general craziness of trying to get through the teenage years without my needing to go through therapy. One of the lessons he'd teach, not that I signed up for the course, had to do with comparing real life with what you see on TV.

We watched a few shows as a family, even though Mom and Dad sometimes only gave half their attention while reading a book or looking at a smartphone, and these typically were family friendly sitcoms where a high schooler was the lead character. In most of the episodes, the teen was either dating, breaking up, getting back together, or generally just freaking out about some love interest. Once, Dad felt the need to point it out as an example of TV not reflecting the real world. "Don't ever think you have to be constantly dating someone to be normal," he said. "I spent half of high school worrying there was something wrong with me whenever I wasn't in a relationship, without stopping to notice that most of my friends weren't either. It was torture."

One might wonder what all of that has to do with the question of whether or not I hated my sisters.

Well, in the same sense that every TV teen is dating, it seems like every TV family is composed of the exact same cast of characters. The dad is a bumbling idiot who can't tie his shoes without setting the house on fire, yet somehow landed a wife who not only is a million times better looking than he is, but always manages to set things exactly right in the end. Every teen girl is crazy about boys, and every teen boy is just flat-out crazy. And then there's the younger sibling. Oh, yes...the younger sibling. Equal parts wise and hilarious, this is the seven year-old who takes a break from building a nuclear reactor in order to deliver the perfect line that absolutely roasts the inept older brother, as the producers smash the "LAUGH" button. If a kid like that existed in real life, he'd get a wedgie to the moon.

And, of course, the TV siblings always fight and argue. Well, that part's not too far off from real life, based on what I've seen of my friends' families, but it just wasn't the case in my house. My sisters were goofier than a clown on a sugar buzz, but they were all right.

Emily was in fifth grade, and Angela in fourth. If my family was on a TV show, the girls would be constantly competing with each other. In reality, they're each other's best friend. People who meet them often assume that they are twins, not because they look identical but because of how similarly they act. They each had plenty of other friends among their classmates, but outside of school, they would prefer to hang out together.

An older brother is supposed to wish his sisters were boys but I got along with them pretty well. I didn't really remember when either one was born, but I'm told I was really upset at first that I wouldn't have a younger brother. It was lucky for me that I didn't, since that meant I got a room to myself. We had only three bedrooms in our house, so the girls shared one of them. It was bigger than mine but obviously I had more space with one fewer bed and stuff like that.

So even though it would have been sweet to boss around a little brother, the girls were pretty fun to have around. They were exceptionally odd kids who got obsessed with different things, which usually involved a scheme to get rich enough to buy a horse ranch after high school. Yes, they could be a pain in the butt every once in a while, but we didn't get in each other's way around the house. That's mostly because they stayed in their room, doing whatever it is that they decided was the most important thing in the world at that time. You'd only know they were in there when one of them would yell at the other, but it would usually be something that only added to the mystery of what was going on. Once I walked by on the way to my room and heard Emily shout, "Don't fart in the closet! You're gonna stink up my clothes!"

A few years ago, they got hooked on knitting. The mom of one of Angela's friends came into her class one day as a sort of parent's version of show-and-tell. Angela had always been good at math whenever it involved money, so she decided that for every dollar she spent on yarn, she could sell twenty dollars' worth of hats and scarves. Emily, despite being older, was always eager to follow. So for about half a year they kept busy, locked in their room, and actually did a pretty good job selling their knitted stuff around the neighborhood, although they probably fell a little short of saving enough to buy that ranch. The hat they gave me for Christmas that year fell apart in about a month, so there's a reason I never saw their fashions being worn around town anymore.

They'd roll through a new fad every so often, but almost every day during summer or after school, they'd keep busy in their room. Their latest obsession was learning magic tricks after Emily got a wizard kit for her birthday. Their big goal was to put on shows at the local auditorium and earn a bunch of money once they became good enough for a public performance. Once they mastered a new trick, they'd come running out to show it to me and my parents, and I had to admit they were getting pretty good. I sometimes had no idea how they did it. They were usually really stubborn about showing me exactly how a certain trick worked, but they were more willing to teach me a few general techniques, like how to force someone to pick a certain playing card from a deck without letting them realize you were actually making the choice for them, or how to "palm" a card. That's when you very gently grab something with the inside of your hand without bending your fingers, so that when people see the back of your open hand, they don't notice that you're actually holding something. I got pretty good at that.

Once I managed to convince them to teach me one of their more impressive card tricks from start to finish. I tried it out with my friends but screwed it up. Not only did I fail to force the right card on Nate, but the wrong card fluttered to the floor before it was time for the big reveal. I think it failed because I was supposed to be wearing long sleeves.

So while my sisters were living their happy little lives in their room for the most part, it's not like they were allergic to the outdoors or to other people. In fact, Emily got to play volleyball for the school team now that she was in fifth grade. And that would give me an opportunity for my first service hours.

Throughout the volleyball season, parents were asked to sign up for at least one shift to sell snacks and drinks during the games being played at our school gym. Now that Emily was playing volleyball, my mom did the same thing she would during my basketball seasons, which is to take her turn early in the season in order to get it over with. I guess I know where I got that trait. And since she always wanted to watch and cheer from the bleachers during her own kids' games, she'd volunteer during games played by St. Mary's teams from any of the other grades.

Mom agreed that I could join her and count those two hours

toward my Saints project, even though there wouldn't be much actual work. That made it a good deal for me, despite having to get up early on a Saturday to walk the five blocks to school and set up before the first game at 8:00 a.m. I woke up tired, having stayed up past midnight playing video games in my room, and with a head full of snot. Since it was the middle of September, it was hard to know whether it was the last of my summer allergies, or the start of a head cold. I felt okay otherwise, so after clearing my nose by blowing a pint of gunk into a few tissues, I threw on some clothes and ran to the front door before my mom even had to yell for me.

It was going to be a warm day again, but the morning was still cool as we took the fifteen-minute walk to school without much conversation. I think my mom also would have preferred a lazy morning at home, but once we got to school, she cheerfully greeted the school's athletic director who'd unlocked the building, gathered supplies from a storage closet, and began brewing pots of coffee while I dragged out a table that would serve as the concession stand in the corner of the gym. Her friend Mrs. Maroney showed up a moment later and fired up the popcorn maker. After a few minutes of setting up the other snacks and the money drawer, we were ready for business.

Mrs. Maroney was my friend Nate's mom. The ladies knew each other since before we were born, but the experience of raising boys at the same time only made them closer. That made Nate my oldest friend, since we'd been spending time together as families for our entire lives.

Meanwhile, girls from both sixth-grade teams had been filing in, already in uniform, and after throwing their duffle bags and water bottles behind their bench, would join their teammates warming up on the court. There were fewer adults than kids,

16

since it seemed that some of the moms had given rides to their own daughters plus one or two other players. I guess a bunch of other parents were as excited about an early Saturday grade school volleyball game as I was. There were also a few assorted grandparents and siblings, including Rachel Juarez and Grace Grant, both of whom were ninth graders who graduated from St. Mary's last year. They each had a sister on the sixth-grade team, and were sitting together well off to the side at a safe distance from the ears of any adults. I didn't exactly have a crush on either of them, but they were cute enough to motivate me to attempt to impress them.

Blowing my nose for about the three hundredth time that morning, I counted a total of around thirty people in the bleachers chatting among themselves, not paying attention to the warmups on the court as the players were practicing their serves. That was their mistake, to my great delight, as errant serves would head straight into the bleachers and bop people in the head. I know I shouldn't have found that as hilarious as I did, but these girls were still too little and weak to really blast someone in the face. That wouldn't be as funny. Maybe.

Mom and Mrs. Maroney continued to talk over their coffee, and did a nice job pretending not to be irritated when their conversation was interrupted by a customer. Fortunately for them, few people seemed interested in a bag of popcorn for breakfast. In the minutes before the start of the match, a couple of moms waltzed over for their own cups of coffee. I'd take their dollar while Mrs. Maroney poured and served. One little kid decided for some reason to sprint from his seat until he was approximately four centimeters from slamming his skull against the edge of the table. He handed me a dollar for a candy bar, obviously in need of even more sugar in his bloodstream, and went tearing back to where he and his dad were sitting. I smiled, wondering if the kid would have been allowed to buy candy if his female parent was there instead.

With the game about to start, I knew that he'd be the last customer for a long while. It would be a slow morning. A boring morning.

"Hey Mom, is it okay if I watch the game from the bleachers?" I asked. "I'll come back if I see it's getting busy."

"Up to you," was her reply as she waved me off, so with my handheld video game in one back pocket of my shorts, and a few tissues stuffed in the other, I trotted along the first row of bleachers as the teams started taking their positions for the first serve. My plan was to head to the top row where the only game I'd be watching was the one on my screen, but I'd strategically take the steps that would have me walk by Rachel and Grace on my way there.

The referee blew the whistle to signal the server to start, but the ninth graders were no more invested in the game than I was, and instead were huddled together in some secret conversation. A few steps before I reached the girls, I quickly snorted everything in my nose back up to where it belonged so I wouldn't embarrassingly drip snot in front of them.

"Oh, hey," I said, in an intriguingly low but nonchalant tone, as if surprised to have suddenly stumbled upon them.

"Hey Jack," said Grace politely despite my interruption. "How do ya like finally being the big kid at St. Mary's?"

I took that to mean, "Hello, handsome. I've missed you terribly since starting high school, and hope you will spend the next ten minutes delighting me with your presence while I stare dreamily into your gorgeous eyes."

Well she wasn't going to get ten minutes, because I only

got as far as "Yeah this place is lame but it's cool to..." before a sneeze erupted without warning. I quickly threw my head into the inside of my left elbow just in time, glad that I wore a long-sleeve shirt and relieved that I hadn't sprayed directly into the girls' faces. But I thought for a moment that I had a bigger problem on my hands, because the force of my sneeze brought me dangerously close to passing gas at the same time. By the grace of all that is holy, I held it in. At least I thought I had; I was pretty sure I didn't feel or hear anything, and there wasn't much noise around us besides a crazy mom whooping at every play like she had bet her life savings on the game. But when I gathered my composure and turned back to face the girls, Rachel's face was contorted into look of horror. It lasted less than a second, but it was definitely there, while Grace was looking straight down, trembling with the unmistakable movement of someone trying to keep from laughing.

Maybe the unthinkable did happen after all, but was attacking a sense other than sound. Slowly as to keep from being obvious, I took a long breath through my nose and surveyed for possible damage. Despite being stuffed up, I felt confident that I hadn't polluted the air.

But something was going on, and guessing that perhaps the zipper of my shorts was open, I muttered a quick "Going great, good to see you" and hurried to the top row of an empty section of bleachers, taking two steps at a time. Confused upon seeing that my fly was indeed zipped shut, I pulled my video game from my pocket, sat down with my feet up on the seat in front of me, and put my elbows on my knees in game-playing position. And as I did that, I finally saw it. A large, thick glob of wet, lime-green snot stuck to the inside of my sleeve.

I shot a quick glance down at Rachel and Grace, who were

19

leaning on each as they shook with laughter. After pulling a tissue from my pocket, I cleaned up my sleeve, resisting the angry urge to throw the tissue down through the gaps in the bleachers to the floor below for someone else to pick up. I buried my head in my game and shut off the world around me.

The volleyball match ended in less than an hour, so I headed down to the concession stand, this time walking across the top bleacher and down a different set of stairs far from where Rachel and Grace sat, to help out with the customers between games. Our two-hour shift meant my mom and I would work during the next game, too, which was being played by the eighth-grade team. It would be fun to watch my classmates, and I decided I might even cheer for them. It wasn't much busier than it was earlier in the morning, so I went back to my seat just before the next game started, actually paying attention this time. Both teams had some really good athletes, but our girls pulled out a win in a close match.

I went back over to the concession stand to finish my shift. There wasn't any reason to clean up, since the stand would stay open for two additional games, and be run by a new set of parents that had already shown up. I sold a few sodas and bags of popcorn while waiting for my mom to say her goodbyes to Mrs. Maroney and the other adults, and we were on our way home.

With a few cups of coffee in her, my mom was a little more talkative. "I don't mind helping out with the concession stand, but it's nice to get my volunteer duty over with," she said.

"Yeah," I agreed, "and I've got ten percent of my Saints hours done."

"More like ten minutes," she laughed.

I was feeling less agreeable. "I was there the whole time! It's not my fault there weren't more people there. And you said I could watch the games."

"I said it was your choice, and the choice you made was to sit on your rump all morning."

I wasn't going to fight it anymore. If I was certain of one thing, it's that I wouldn't win that argument. And if I was certain of another, it's that I wouldn't be finishing my service hours anytime soon.

3

Truth and Consequences

"So what makes you think there even is a God in the first place?"

It was an odd question to hear coming from a priest.

Father Drew had come to talk to our religion class, supposedly to give us a pep talk about the Saints project. Religion was usually taught by Ms. Garcia, our homeroom teacher who also handled literature and social studies for both the seventh and eighth grade. But once every couple of weeks, one of the priests would pay a visit, walking over from the nearby rectory. That was the house where our two parish priests lived on the other side of the church, which itself was next to the school building. Father Robert was the pastor, the priest who was in charge, and he'd been at St. Mary's for several years. We usually had a second, younger priest who would be assigned to our church for a few years to gain experience before being sent to another parish to replace a pastor who had retired.

And Father Drew was brand new, having just become a priest the previous June, with St. Mary's as his first assignment. I'd met him during the summer, since I was an altar boy at Mass about every other week, and he was the celebrating priest about half of those times.

I knew a few things about him. He grew up in a bigger city about thirty miles away, and went to the university there. We just called it "State U." That's where I hoped to go to college, but more importantly, it's the school whose sports teams we root for in this part of the state. While at the university, he finally decided he was called to be a priest after thinking about it for several years. He wanted to finish college first, so before entering the seminary he graduated with a degree in biochemistry. Something about that surprised me but I wasn't sure why. Maybe I assumed priests were people who grew up in a sort of separate world and only studied the Bible.

He was probably in his mid-to-upper 20s and seemed like a regular guy, a lot like a cousin of mine who was about that age. I'd sometimes see him shooting a basketball by himself or with a couple of kids on the playground after school, and when I was biking around the neighborhood I might notice him jogging along the sidewalk. That was probably a good idea, since I knew that the older ladies in the church felt it was their collective duty to stockpile the rectory with homemade cakes and casseroles. He and Father Robert would both have to be triathletes to burn all the calories that were dropped off on their doorstep.

I also knew he was a nice guy. He was one of those people who asks you questions about yourself when he first meets you, and actually seems to be interested in your responses. My parents liked him a lot, although the only thing they really had to go on was some small talk after Mass; that, and his sermons. I must have liked his preaching too, because every time he finished, I found myself realizing that I had paid attention to the whole thing. Earlier in the summer, I could tell by his voice that he was a little nervous, knowing that he was making his first impression on everyone in the pews.

He was clearly not as nervous speaking to the less judgmental ears of my classmates as he repeated his question.

"No, seriously," he said with a half-smile as he scanned across the room at the blank faces looking back at him. "How do you know there's a God?"

A voice from a few seats behind me piped up, slowly singing a song lyric I hadn't heard since preschool. "For – the – Bi - ble – tells – me - so..."

I recognized Peyton's voice without needing to turn around, while a few snickers emerged from around the room.

"Is that your answer?" asked Father Drew, still smiling without any hint of annoyance.

"Well...yeah," Peyton answered, sounding a little embarrassed for being put on the spot despite having begged for the attention. "It's all in the Bible."

"Okay, yes, that's true enough," Father said, getting a little more energized now that he got someone talking. "But why should we believe it just because it's written down? There are all sorts of books with made-up stories."

I wasn't sure where this was going, or what it had to do with the Saints project, but I was on the verge of finding it mildly interesting.

Without waiting for an answer from Peyton, Father Drew continued. "Who else has an answer?"

Olivia Torres raised her hand. "Because everything has to come from something," she said. "The universe couldn't have created itself; it had to have been caused by something outside of it."

Father Drew seemed impressed, but we all remembered talking about that in class a few years ago. Well, those of us who paid attention did.

"That's a fine answer," Father responded. "We can use scientific observation to find clues to a creator. How many of you know that it was a priest who developed the Big Bang theory?" Just a few people raised their hands, even though most of us knew that too. "Anyone who says you can only believe in either science or God is just completely wrong. They're not opposites. The Church has made huge contributions to science over the centuries and still does today. Other answers?"

"Yeah, I know there's a God because Jesus died and rose from the dead," Carlos blurted without bothering to raise his hand. "Plus there were all his miracles and other stuff."

Father grinned at that last part, then said, "Yes, but hold that thought. We'll get to Jesus in a minute. Pretend you never heard anything about Jesus. Would there be any other reason to believe in God?"

A long silence followed, but my guess was that it had more to do with kids worrying about being seen as uncool rather than having nothing else to add.

After a moment, Mike Ryan, leader of the Roundies, reluctantly raised his hand. Mike's family was serious about their religion. You'd never go to any church event without seeing his family. His parents even led Bible Study groups, so Mike knew more about Catholicism than the rest of us put together. He was just sort of shy about the topic. I don't think he was embarrassed by his faith, but he didn't want to be seen as a show-off, like how Alycia Franklin always screamed out math answers before anyone else had a chance. So even though Mike could have been part of the conversation since the start, he only weighed in after no one else spoke up.

"Yes, Mike?" Father Drew invited. Of course, I observed, he

25

knew him and his family by name.

"The moral law," Mike quietly answered.

"Tell me what you mean by that," said Father Drew, who surely knew exactly what Mike meant by that.

Mike took a deep breath and thought a while before answering. "We're all guided by a moral law that gives us a sense of what's right and what's wrong, or at least which thing is more right than the other," he said. "It's there in our conscience, or the voice in our heads that tells us that we ought to save the person in the burning building instead of run away from it."

"But you're just choosing between two competing evolutionary instincts, right?" Father challenged him. "Your personal survival instinct competing with the sense that we developed over thousands of years to support the needs of the tribe, right?"

"Well, no," said Mike hesitantly, like he was wondering if he was answering a rhetorical question, or actually arguing with a priest for probably the first time in his life. "I'm not just talking about those two instincts. There's a third thing that's greater than those. Something else that helps you to judge which of those two instincts you ought to follow, even if you choose the thing you shouldn't."

"But how can you call it a law when people don't always act the same way?" Father pressed.

"Well, yeah, we still have the freedom to decide whether to follow the moral law, to choose either good or bad," Mike said. "It's like a code of conduct, where everyone understands that there's a certain way we should behave that we call 'good'. We know there's a such a thing as good and bad, and we know deep inside that we ought to do the thing that is good."

"Isn't that just a matter of how you were taught to behave?"

Father asked.

"No," Mike replied, "because even people who do bad things *know* they're doing bad things and *like* to do bad things *because* they're bad things. Someone who's mean to other people still knows the moral law but doesn't care that he's breaking it. Or sometimes people do the wrong thing but it's for reasons they think are good. 'I stole from one person to help another and that was generous of me.' 'I'm totally greedy but I earned it so it's fair'. 'I insulted him because he made fun of me first so that's justice.' 'I punched him because he cheated from me and that's not fair.' He's using one part of the moral law to defend why he's breaking another part of the moral law, and he expects us to understand it because the moral law is in all of us. You can't explain where that comes from just by saying that our parents or our ancestors taught us to be fair and kind."

"Why not?" Father asked. "Isn't it just our parents or our society that teaches us those things?"

"Yeah, but it's more than just learning good manners, because that doesn't explain what makes those things in the moral law *good*," Mike responded. "If I ask why it's good to be fair, the answer can't just be 'because fairness is good'. Why should I treat people fairly? 'Because it's important to help others.' Why? 'Because helping others is good for civilization'. But why should I rather do the thing that helps someone else or the whole civilization, instead of doing what helps me right now? 'Because that wouldn't be fair.' I mean, you can just go around in circles forever until you accept the idea that there is a moral law *outside of ourselves* that guides our decisions and tells us there's a right and wrong way to behave. It's like an instruction manual that we're all born with. But we didn't write it, and our ancestors didn't write it, so someone else must have."

"Okay, that's a solid start," Father answered, sensing that the conversation was starting to go over the heads of the rest of us, although I thought I mostly kept up. "We could get a lot deeper into that, but that's just one example of what we can call *philosophical* evidence to go with an example of physical evidence we mentioned earlier. And there's a lot more of both those kinds of evidence. So not only can we point to a creator, but a creator who tells us something about his personality by guiding us to behave in a certain way. It's a way we don't always follow, as if something somewhere went wrong a long time ago. So wrong that we needed some extra help to get us back on the right path."

I saw where he was going with that.

"So, what else do we know?" Father continued before gesturing toward Carlos. "You brought up Jesus. What reasons do we have to believe the things we were taught about him?"

"The gospels!" Alycia interrupted, in the same confident way that she'd answer questions about algebra problems.

"But aren't those just more Bible stories that could be made up?" Father challenged.

"Except that they were written by people who knew him, or were told to the writers by people who were there," she replied. "And told to lots of people who would have known if they were lies."

"Yeah, that's kind of important, isn't it?" Father chuckled. "You might hear people discredit the gospels for being written a certain number of years after Jesus' time. That's like saying if your parents tell you a story about when they were kids, it can't possibly be true since they didn't write it down in a book at the time. Anyone else have a reason for believing in Jesus?"

"It fits," said Mike. "All of his teachings fit. And if they didn't,

28

the whole thing would collapse in on itself."

"How do you mean?"

"He said he was the Son of God," Mike said. "If he wasn't, then he lied or was insane, but the rest of what he said and did fits together too well to come from a crazy liar. Someone who's that deranged wouldn't be able to teach so rationally. It's logically impossible. The only likely explanation is that he is who he said he was."

"You'll hear some people ask whether his entire story was just made up," Father added, "but all serious biblical scholars – even those who don't believe Jesus was God – believe the man existed. Anyone else have a reason to believe the gospels?"

What seemed like a minute passed before someone answered in a voice that sounded a lot like mine.

"The apostles," came from a voice that was indeed mine, to my great surprise. I really didn't intend to be a part of this, but the words came out before I even realized it.

"What about the apostles?" Father asked.

"Well, like Alycia said, they would have known if it was true or not," I said about the closest followers of Jesus. "You can say the gospels are all made up, but they would have known if Jesus was a liar, they would have known if he never really performed any miracles, and they would have known if Jesus never rose from the dead. But instead of going back to their jobs and families after he died, they kept preaching what they were taught by him and what they saw for themselves. And they..." I stopped myself from saying something I worried I'd regret.

Father noticed my hesitation but encouraged me to go on.

"And," I restarted, "not to be disrespectful, but these guys sorta were losers."

Laughing but intrigued, Father asked, "In what way, and why

29

does that matter?"

"I mean, these were just normal guys, right?" I went on. "Mostly fishermen, I think, but just a bunch of random everyday guys that didn't have any real education. My dad and his friends can't keep a fantasy football league going for more than a couple of seasons, so how could the apostles be inspired to build a worldwide church that's lasted for two thousand years unless what they experienced was exactly what the gospels say? For us now, we still need to have some faith, but the apostles would have known for themselves whether it was all true."

I'd like to say this was an original thought, but I picked it up somewhere in recent years, whether from one of my parents or at school. Regardless, it was the one thing that always stuck with me most.

Knowing he had me on a roll, Father challenged me.

"But people were simpler back then," Father said. By now I was on to his tactic, so I knew he was making arguments he didn't believe himself. "They could have been fooled by things that weren't really miracles, or been hallucinating when they thought they saw Jesus after the crucifixion. They didn't understand the science of death and the impossibility of resurrection."

"Of course they did!" I nearly shouted, getting way more animated than I ever expected but continuing almost on autopilot. "They knew enough to know that people didn't just come back from the dead. That's why it was such a big deal to them! They saw Jesus raise the dead and be raised himself, and that's why they knew he was God! They understood it so well that they left everything behind to go all over the world and tell everyone about it even if it meant getting thrown in jail or beaten up or killed. You wouldn't do that if you weren't completely shocked and convinced by what you saw! But yeah, I guess Jesus was just a con artist who invented the most influential religious teachings in history, then fooled thousands of people with the most amazing magic tricks the world has ever seen, then caught a huge break when the world's first-ever case of mass hallucination tricked hundreds of people into thinking they saw him, talked to him, and heard him preach for a month after they saw him dead and buried. And it was all just a ridiculously huge set of coincidences that all happened around the same one guy. *That's* a better explanation for Christianity? Come on!"

I slumped back into my chair, not having realized that I had gotten half out of my seat in the middle of my rant. I would have thought I only imagined all that coming out of my mouth, but the faces of twenty five classmates staring back at me in silence told me otherwise.

Clap. Clap. Clap. That was the slow, sarcastic applause of Peyton from the back of the room. As with his voice, I didn't need to see it to know it was him.

Father Drew ignored him, but didn't hand me the medal I frankly thought I deserved. Rather, looking at the clock to see that the end of the class period was approaching, he quickly moved on.

"And now we have historical evidence on top of our philosophical evidence and our physical evidence," he said. "But it's really only the beginning. There's so much more. You can spend years learning more if you like. But even if you don't, what I want to leave you with is the knowledge that there are answers to these questions. Not just the existence of God or the truth of the gospels, but also the reasons behind the teachings of the Church.

"Look, I know we were supposed to talk about your Saints

project today, but we're talking about this instead because it's really important. All of you are going to question things as you get older, especially after you encounter more people in this world who don't believe what you believe, either because they never learned it themselves, or because they decided it wasn't real or important to them. Some of them are going to question your beliefs, maybe out of honest curiosity but sometimes out of hostility or as a way to mock you for being so stupid as to actually be a practicing Catholic.

"You've all obviously been taught pretty well so far. You know a lot more than you did when you were in kindergarten, but it's important to take the time to keep learning, or at least to go find the answers to questions that you'll have. Trust me, the answers are there. Most of the criticisms you'll hear, even from adults, are kindergarten arguments. 'If God was real, he would have heard my prayer to get a better-paying job.' Do your parents give you everything you ask for? Have you ever noticed that once in a while, it seems like they know a little more about what's best for you, even when you don't understand why they just won't give you what you think will make you happy?"

I thought back to when my sister Angela was about three years old, and every time my mom asked what she wanted for lunch, she'd yell "CAKE! CAKE! CAKE!" That didn't work out for her either.

"Here's another one," Father continued. "'I believe in *science*, not religion. Religion is for those poor little uneducated people.' That's my personal favorite, especially when you see some people feeling the need to proclaim their superiority on little signs in their front lawn. But it's ludicrous. Religion isn't in conflict with science. Faith isn't the opposite of reason. That's what's known as a false choice. It's like analyzing a sculpture

32

and deciding it developed out of nothing because if there was an artist, you'd see him in the sculpture. But a creator exists *outside* of the thing he created. Sort of obvious, right? That's what I mean by kindergarten arguments. God doesn't live in outer space for us to find with a telescope. Of course, we believe our creator *did* choose to come into his creation as a man at a specific point in time, but all the evidence for that gets ignored by these same people. So much for believing in science."

That was a pretty good burn, I thought. No wonder my dad liked him.

"Some questions are harder to answer," Father said. "Questions like, 'If there was a God, why do bad things happen to good people? A loving God wouldn't allow any suffering in the world.'"

Father's arm shot toward the wall near the door, as he pointed at the crucifix hanging there. "You think he doesn't know anything about suffering?"

I looked again at the crucifix I'd walked by every day without hardly noticing, an image so common to me that it was easy to ignore, of a man beaten nearly to death before being nailed to a cross to finish him off. And after years of poverty, persecution, betrayal. Yeah, that was suffering.

"It's hard for us to understand God's ways," Father said, "so some of these aren't unreasonable questions, but they're not *new* questions. Every generation includes some people who think they've come up with a brand-new refutation of Christianity without knowing it was already addressed and debunked, maybe even hundreds of years ago. But you won't be able to answer or defend against those arguments if you only know kindergarten-level stuff yourselves.

"You need to know what the Church teaches, and to separate

that from what some other Christians believe. Lots of non-Catholic Christians come up with some nutty ideas, and then the world lumps us all together and thinks the rest of us Christians believe that too. No, the Catholic Church doesn't teach that the universe is only 4000 years old. No, we don't think every Bible story is *literally* true, but that its authors sometimes use what are called allegories to explain those truths. So we don't believe that there were literally only six human days between the creation of the universe and mankind."

And some of the arguments are less serious, I thought to myself. Sometime around Christmas last year, my mom was telling us about a guy she worked with who took it upon himself to point out that Christians have no way of knowing that Jesus was born on December 25, as if that was some shocking revelation. Gosh, thanks, I had no idea. I guess I'll become a pagan now, except that the Church doesn't think it really matters exactly when his actual birthday is.

"So many of the claims you'll hear come from people who really don't have a clue about what the Church teaches," Father said, "and they don't *want* to know more even if you try to correct them. They're far more close-minded than they accuse us of being. Worse, they're often former Catholics who were poorly taught and aren't interested in learning anything else about what ought to be the most important thing in their lives. They're throwing away their lives and taking others with them. Like them, you'll have questions and doubts in life. That's okay. But dig deeper. The answers are all there if you take the time to look for the truth.

"And Christianity is true. It's not just an opinion. It's not a political party, it's not just some organization or a cause that does nice work, and it sure isn't just another lifestyle choice.

If it's true, then it's a billion times more important than any of those things. It means that you – and every other human, whether they are Christian or not – are a child of God. That should be the most important fact in your life every day. You were created by the same one God who made the planet Jupiter. Think about that. But you're far more special than the stars and the planets because you have a soul that will exist for eternity, and God wants you to be with him now and for all time, if you will only choose him. You are Christian, and that identity is who you are, more than any other thing about yourself. Nothing in your life could possibly be more important than that. Got it?"

I joined most of the class in nodding in agreement, while a few others seemed to be daydreaming about lunch.

"Okay, let's wrap this up," Father said. "So, we all now have 100% complete assurance in the existence of God, right?" He smiled at a sea of blank faces. "Of course it's not that easy. There is an element of faith that's required, but even *that* is what we'd expect from a God who loves us and wants us to love him. It's not really love if he forces us into it. He could show himself in a way that terrifies us into believing in him, but that's not his way. He wants us to make a free choice on our own. But wouldn't it be so much easier on us just to make himself visible? Well he already did. Remember? That's what this was all about," he said, again pointing toward the wall at the image of Jesus.

4

Custodiots

I always thought I'd be a lot more excited about volunteer work if it was something I got paid to do. Yes, I understood that by definition it would then no longer be *volunteer* work, but it would have been nice to get something for the effort. Pay or no pay, though, there have been times when I felt like I actually made a little difference in someone's life. I suppose sometimes that's enough.

A few summers ago, Nate and I hung outside the grocery store one day offering to help elderly people load their bags into their cars. Now, to be honest, the idea was sparked by a little bit of boredom and a much larger hope that we'd collect a bunch of tips from everyone. A few dollars multiplied by a couple dozen old folks could have meant real money. And we did earn several bucks, but really the best part was that more than half the time, the people reacted with a sense of pleasant surprise, touched that we were offering to make a kind gesture with no *obvious* expectation of getting something in return. You could see in their faces that we brought some joy to their days, and it was gratifying even if it was only half an hour before we got chased off the parking lot by an older kid from the store who was collecting shopping carts.

Most of the time, though, my volunteer work consisted of tagging along with one of my parents, helping at some fundraiser for the school, the church, or the Men of St. Mary's, which as one might guess was a group that my dad and a bunch of other men from the parish belonged to. I still knew I was helping to raise money for important things, but that felt a little less satisfying than directly helping a person in need.

Well, a few weeks after the fiasco at the volleyball concession stand, I was about to get my first real "Saints in Service" project hours, but there would be no money, no grateful faces, and no warm feelings.

It was the beginning of October, and Nate and I had signed up for our week of custodial work after school. That would give me about five hours to count toward my Saints project; six, if we took a little extra time each day. A few of the guys had already taken their turns doing that work in the previous weeks. I knew which week Boone and Peyton "worked", since the bathroom floors were still full of puddles every morning from their sloppy mopping job the day before. But they all made it sound like it was an hour each day of pretty easy work. The plan was that Nate and I would each take one of the two wings of the school building, which each had four classrooms to sweep and a pair of bathrooms to mop. We'd empty the waste baskets into a larger trash barrel that we'd wheel around and leave by the custodians' workroom for them to take care of the next morning, vacuum the carpeted library and administrative offices just once at some point during the week, and that would be it. The custodians took care of everything else during the course of their workday, but would head for home shortly after we started our shift, locking

37

the doors so we would be able to leave but not get back in.

And having the school to ourselves was an interesting experience. We weren't supposed to start cleaning until 4:00 p.m., after all the kids had cleared out and the teachers had either wrapped up their end-of-day work or packed it up to take home with them. Nate and I would be the only ones left in the building, though we had to be careful that none of the teachers was still hanging around later than expected. Boone found that out the hard way one day when he steered his broom from the hall into what he thought was an empty third-grade classroom, yelling to no one in particular, "And how big a mess did you little monsters leave?," only to look up and see Mr. Salvatore still at his desk.

When the school day ended on the Monday of our volunteer week, Nate and I headed outside to the playground to kill time until 4:00 p.m. This was always my favorite time of year, with my late summer allergies behind me for good, football on TV every weekend, the Halloween atmosphere growing by the day, and the first basketball practice for my school team on the horizon. It was sunny and chilly, and I thought it was glorious.

A few of our classmates joined us in shooting baskets with the ball Mason brought every day, but eventually headed for their homes after a not-very-serious debate over who would be the lead scorer on our team this season. It was always Tyler, still about six inches taller than us and nearly all of the kids on the other teams.

Nate and I reported to the custodian's office and found Mr. K, whose actual name would take me a hundred tries to spell correctly. He led us to the janitor's closet in the middle of the two wings of the building, described the chores we already knew how to do, pointed out the brooms, mops, and buckets, and left us to get to work. I reached across a bolted-in metal ladder that led to a hatch that opened out onto the roof, and grabbed a broom. It was the type with a frilly head that was about three feet wide, which meant I could finish my side of the hallway in about four passes. Like I was told by my friends, it would only take a half hour to wrap it all up. What I did with the rest of that time would be up to me.

"Have fun!" Nate said sarcastically (as if there's any other adverb that applies to things said by teenage boys), and made his way down the hall along one side of the tile floor. I turned in the opposite direction and looked ahead at the corridor before me. These were the fifth-through-eighth-grade rooms, two on each side of the hall. Beyond those were two restrooms, across from each other near an exit. My plan was to sweep one side of the hall, hitting the classrooms and restroom on one side and then the other, and make my way back to the janitor's closet to swap the broom for a mop and bucket of water to clean the restroom floors. I'd clear out the waste baskets and call it a day. Although the main office and teachers' lounge were on my wing, I didn't have to vacuum them every day so I planned to put that off until Friday.

For each student, there was a small desk of the sort that has a little open compartment underneath it to put books, folders, and other supplies. I chuckled to myself knowing that Nate would be in rooms where littler kids were smearing paste and boogers and who knows what else on their desks and chairs, but of course we weren't expected to have to clean that up and risk touching any of their disgusting-ness. Unlike in the younger grades where desks were arranged in little clusters of four or six, the rooms in this wing were placed in neat rows facing forward so as to protect the students from the horror of actually having to face each other.

Between the dozens of chair and desk legs, there wasn't much room to maneuver my broom, but I can honestly say I did my best. Well, my best would have been to set all the chairs on top of the desks before sweeping the floor beneath, but I wasn't about to get carried away. Besides, there's no way any of the other guys before me did even half as good a job as I did, and I didn't notice us drowning in a sea of dust bunnies during the weeks they worked.

Finding myself taking a little bit of pride in my work and striving to do a decent job, it was several minutes longer than I'd expected before I went back to the janitor's closet, transferred my fuzzy collection from a dustpan into the trash bin, and turned on the water to fill a mop bucket from a hose connected to a large sink. Over the sound of the rushing water, I thought I heard a noise down the hall behind me. It dawned on me that being alone in the school could be a little creepy if you let your imagination get to you. I stepped back into the hallway for a look down Nate's side of the school, but the emptiness told me he must have been sweeping inside one of the rooms. Since I saw the other bucket still in its place in the closet, I knew he hadn't gotten around to mopping yet.

When the bucket was about half full, I added some liquid soap, plunged a mop into the pail, and used the handle to push and steer it out of the closet and back up my hallway to the restrooms, starting with the boys'.

There's a moment in almost every horror movie when some girl slowly walks toward a door to investigate the creepy sound she heard coming from inside a closet, or whatever. Even though a normal girl would be too smart to do anything but call the cops or run from the house, "movie girl" presses on, clearly terrified, not knowing whether it will be her pet cat or a serial killer that jumps out from the other side of the door.

As I swished my mop back and forth along the boy's bathroom floor in front of the urinals and made my way toward the toilet stalls along the back wall, I was that girl. There were four stalls in all, none of them locked of course, but with closed doors that rested against their latches. I would have to push each door open and run the mop around the tile surrounding the toilet.

I'd learned that humans become increasingly afraid of things the more likely they are to happen. So a serial killer was of no concern to me. But from experience, I knew that it was all too possible that I would open the door to at least one unflushed toilet.

I'd always been pretty defensive when girls talk about how gross we boys are, but there are times when the ladies have a point. I can be as big a slob as anyone, but I've never understood how anyone could walk away from the bathroom without flushing. Is it really too much trouble? I always used my foot to kick the handle, so it can't be a germ thing. And even worse were the kids that walk out of the bathroom without washing their hands. That is apparently something you don't necessarily grow out of, because I'd seen all sorts of adult men doing the same thing. Sometimes I wondered why I even bothered myself, since my clean hands would end up grabbing a door handle touched by a bunch of cavemen who exited before me.

So I used my foot to push open the first stall, my eyes squinted so that if there was some unavoidable horror to behold, I'd only vaguely realize it was lurking there, and I could finish the job pretending all was well.

But there was nothing there, and my guard was let down as I moved from stall to stall. Hopeful that the school was celebrating "Act Like a Civilized Human Being Day," I began to open the last stall door.

"RRRRAAAAHHHH!!!!!!!!!" came a scream from a shadowy creature hovering over the toilet. I jumped backward, nearly slipping on the wet tile but finding my balance. With my heart pounding, I looked up just as I was moving to begin a sprint toward the door. Standing on the toilet seat was Nate, delighted at making me look like a fool.

"You jerk," I said with a chuckle. My smile was an attempt to let him know he hadn't gotten me as bad as he did, even if my absolute freak-out indicated otherwise.

"Oh, man, that was awesome!," Nate said as he jumped off the toilet, then slipped on the tile and lurched forward until his momentum was stopped by his head cracking against the side of the stall. "AHHH!"

"You deserved that," I laughed, as he rubbed the pain off his skull.

"Fine, we're even."

"That's what you think," I said, already formulating a plan to get way more than just *even*. "Are you anywhere close to being done?" After responding that all he had left was to mop his set of restrooms, I said, "Hurry it up. I don't feel like staying past five today."

Nate held the doors for me while I rolled the bucket across the hall from the boys' room to the girls', then he turned down toward the janitor's closet to get his own pail. Being in the girls' bathroom was a little weird, to be honest. Something about it just felt cleaner, if that makes sense. Like when secondhand clothes are called "gently used", their bathroom just seemed less abused and beaten up. Grudgingly realizing it was more evidence that boys are pigs, I made quick work of the floor, went to the janitor's closet to rinse the mop and dump the water down the drain, and wheeled the large trash bin back along the same route, collecting the contents of the small waste baskets from each of the same rooms, noticing with an unexpected sense of satisfaction that the floors looked obviously better than before.

Rolling the bin back to the janitor's closet, I placed it in the corner where I'd found it. Nate must have still been mopping, and while we didn't think to plan a spot to meet once we were ready to go home, it made sense to wait for him out in the hallway right there, where he would finish his chores as I did.

Or I could wait for him *inside* the closet, I thought. Shutting the door behind me, I grabbed the metal ladder with one hand, flicked the light off with the other, then in complete darkness climbed up about eight ladder rungs until even my feet were higher than the head of someone standing on the floor.

About ten minutes went by, long enough for my feet to start hurting from the thick metal bar they were pressed on, and almost long enough for me to wonder if I should reconsider what was about to be an epic scare. Thankfully, before I talked myself out of it, I heard footsteps approaching from outside. I waited for the door to open, and just as his hand reached through the darkness for the light switch, I screamed - and I mean *screamed*...

"NAAAAAAAAAAAAAAAATE!!!!!!!"

With the closet only dimly lit by the light from the hallway, I beamed as he shot his head up with a terrified look on his blood-drained face as if he expected to be attacked by a demon-killer-clown-zombie from the deepest bowels of the netherworld. It was every bit as awesome as I hoped.

Nate found it less awesome. After the split-second it took to recognize me, he took the mop in his hand, slammed it against

43

the wall, and stomped out of the closet. I climbed down the ladder, dumped his mop pail for him, and followed after him, almost but not quite feeling a tinge of regret. Once he pulled himself together, we grabbed our backpacks from Ms. Garcia's room and started the walk home. He was still a little frosty as we walked the two blocks before our paths split, but he'd get over it by the next day.

The remaining days of my weeklong janitor career followed the same pattern and were pretty uneventful. I did find myself getting a little bolder, as if I owned the place and had the authority to snoop around the classrooms. It started in Ms. Hurley's fifth-grade homeroom, where my sister Emily spent most of her days. Emily's desk was neat and orderly, which didn't surprise me, but I figured it was my brotherly duty to peek into the desks around her looking for signs of trouble. I wasn't expecting to find ninja throwing stars or anything like that, but I would've wanted to know if some snot nearby was drawing mean doodles of Emily or something. The worst I found was a ball the size of my fist made up of about a hundred used wads of chewing gum. I guess we all have our hobbies, including this madman.

Toward the end of the week, I was sweeping in my own classroom when a sheet of notepaper in Anna Kemper's desk caught my eye. It was folded up about four times over until it was just the size of a sticky note. On the top side was drawn a heart in red marker, which signaled to me that there was likely some valuable information inside. Anna was inarguably the prettiest girl in our class, and while all of us boys had a crush on her at some point over the years, she was pretty mean and made it clear that she would never lower her standards enough to ever develop feelings for any of us dopes. But maybe that changed, and this was a note she intended to give me the next day, expressing that she could no longer deny her love for me.

With broom handle in one hand, I reached down and grabbed the note just as Mr. K appeared in the doorway. Making sure to appear understandably surprised but not suspiciously guilty, I quickly palmed the note in my hand so that it looked empty to Mr. K. I'd have to remember to thank my sisters later for teaching me that trick.

"Didn't mean to scare you," he shouted in his typical booming voice. "Everything going okay?"

"Oh yeah, just fine," I said. "Had to tie my shoe," I lied, just in case he saw me bent over but also to explain why I was standing still. I congratulated myself for the quick thinking.

"Good deal. You two are doing nice work this week," he said, referring to me and Nate. "Thanks for making my job easier. Have a good one!"

I thanked him for the compliment as he left. When the sound of his footsteps faded, I opened Anna's note. To my disappointment, it was just something Olivia wrote basically telling Anna what a great friend she is. Lame.

Confident that there'd be no more surprises at the door, I pushed the broom to the front of the room and swept around Ms. Garcia's desk. A thought that had occurred to me earlier in the week popped back into my head.

I was pretty sure the bottom left drawer of her desk contained the master copies of our tests, among other things. There was a social studies exam scheduled for the next Monday, and even though I felt like I knew the material well and wouldn't have to study much over the weekend, I figured it would sure be easier if I didn't have to study at all.

I hesitated, looking at the drawer while briefly contemplating the matter. I was going to do the right thing and walk away. There was no question that cheating was wrong, and the thought of invading Ms. Garcia's privacy by rooting through her desk made me more than a little uncomfortable. But "thou shalt not cheat" isn't one of the Ten Commandments, at least not in those words. I'd still be a pretty good Christian, and I wouldn't be sharing the answers with anyone else. And really, I was smart enough to probably ace the test no matter what. All this would do was just help me finish faster.

I shot a quick look at the door to make sure I was alone, reached down and pulled on the drawer. It was locked. I grabbed the broom and walked into the hallway, more relieved than disappointed. I ended up not doing the wrong thing after all, but somehow didn't feel like much of a hero.

5

Pope Me the First

I had a pretty consistent routine after the end of every school day. My mom was usually home, and I'd say a quick hello while she was reading or doing something like yoga or housework. Even though she went back to her job as a nurse a few years earlier when Angela started first grade, it was only part-time and on the condition that her shifts during the school year were limited mostly to weekday mornings and the occasional Saturday. Most Tuesday nights she volunteered at a different kind of clinic, one that offered free counseling to people and families with alcohol or other drug problems, but she never had to leave for that until after we'd eaten dinner together.

My sisters were usually already in their room, having headed directly home from school, anxious to get back to whatever hobby they'd taken up. I'd pass their closed door on the way to my room, pausing only to hear enough to be assured that they made it home safely but often picking up another head-scratching comment. "Don't even *think* about sawing my elephant in half!," I heard Angela yell, and since that frankly wasn't in the top one hundred of the weirdest things I'd heard from them, I continued on to my own room.

I usually waited until after dinner to start on any homework I might have, so on a typical day I spent the time right after school to just hang out and relax. Dad would be home more than an hour later from his job as a financial officer for a manufacturing company, working on budgets and taxes and whatever else it was that finance people did. He'd help Mom finish getting dinner ready, and if I was feeling generous and bored, I'd pitch in.

But I was rarely bored. Ever since I got a smartphone that last summer, I spent a lot of time checking out a bunch of different social media accounts. My parents didn't let me create my own accounts but they didn't mind if I just checked out the platforms that let me view stuff that other people posted, even if I couldn't comment or add my own content.

My favorite influencers were Skip Skip and Belle. They were in their early twenties, I guessed, since they never talked about being in school. Come to think of it, they never talked about having actual jobs either, but they were pretty hilarious. They posted ten-minute videos talking about whatever was going on in the world at the time. Most of what they discussed was just pop culture and not real news, which would have been a more intelligent topic than they were equipped to handle. I had to admit they were a little goofy, but that's what made it entertaining to me. Lots of people must have agreed, because they had a few million followers.

"Hey Skip Nation!" Skip Skip would often start, greeting viewers by the name he made up for them. "Halloween is coming and that means it's time for Skip Skip and Belle's countdown of the scariest movies EVAH!" Belle jumped into the frame wearing a monster mask, and danced around behind Skip

Skip while some creepy music played. Then they ran through their countdown, cracking jokes, and rating each movie on a scale of 1-10 pairs of pants peed. I wondered why anyone would wear more than one pair of pants when watching a movie, but I learned a long time ago that there was no point in thinking harder about it than these two did themselves.

After watching the clip, I always enjoyed scrolling through the viewer comments. Sometimes I found those funnier than anything Skip Skip said. They were definitely more vulgar. I might have "accidentally" failed to show my dad that there was a comments section when he asked to see a few examples of what I was spending my time looking at online. I'm pretty sure he wouldn't have approved of me reading that trash, but he was okay with the Skip Skip videos, knowing that I could be watching a lot worse stuff out there.

"How's Drip Drip today?" came a voice from my doorway. Sounded like Dad was home a little early.

He always had a new lame nickname, much to my annoyance, making sure I never forgot his opinion on social media influencers - and their viewers, for that matter. Few things irritated him more than people he thought were egomaniacs, and he decided that anyone who truly believed he or she had something so incredibly valuable to say that it absolutely needed to be shared with the entire online world landed in that category. I didn't necessarily think he was incorrect.

Dad didn't have a problem with people who share pictures of their vacations or their kids' games or little snippets of their lives with their families and friends. He thought it was nice to stay connected that way, and he posted plenty of stuff like that himself. It was the self-congratulatory ego boosts that drove him nuts, and it wasn't limited to internet posts.

49

If you could make a career out of critiquing bumper stickers the way some people make a living reviewing movies, my dad would be set for life. He didn't mind the ones that supported a sports team or a band or even a politician, despite his thinking little of most of that last group. At least those stickers are pointing toward something other than the driver's own ego, he'd say. But by his logic, when people put one bumper sticker on a car, they're telling the world that it's the most important message they want to share out of a million other options. And some of those messages, he felt, weren't nearly as profound as the drivers seemed to think.

Once he and I were walking through the parking lot of the grocery store, and I pointed out a bumper sticker that had nothing but the quote "I Am an Atheist", followed by the name of the person who apparently proclaimed it. "Hmm. Convincing argument," Dad said sarcastically.

"I don't recognize that name," I said.

"She was a moderately famous actress a long time ago, so I guess we're supposed to be persuaded to rethink the meaning of life," he answered. "She's dead now," he added almost as an afterthought.

"And she was an atheist?" I asked.

"Not no more, she ain't," he said. "That must have come as a surprise to her."

Another time we were traveling on vacation, and Dad was about to pass a minivan on the highway. The entire back window was covered in a white decal that read, "They Told Her She Couldn't, So She Went And Did It. 13.1."

I knew that number was a reference to a half-marathon, and I knew that wasn't going to go by without a comment. Sure enough, Dad, pretending not to have read the entire thing before opening his mouth, said "Hey everybody let's congratulate this lady for curing cancer! Oh, never mind, she went out for a jog one day. My bad."

There were fewer examples of that lately, as Dad said he was trying to be less cynical and judgmental, but I suppose it's hard to change one's personality overnight, or even over a couple years, in his case.

"Skip Skip's just fine," I answered. "He was talking about his list of best Halloween movies."

"If 'Attack of Maniac Clown: Summer Camp Slaughter' isn't in his top three, he has zero credibility," replied Dad, himself a fan of the genre.

"Yeah, I know you don't like him," I said.

"Oh, I just like giving you a hard time," he said. "I'd rather find you reading some classic literature, but I know you study hard and deserve some time away from that. But be careful, okay? The culture today pretty much stinks like a rotting skunk corpse, but I realize I watch plenty of junk that isn't particularly intellectual. Sometimes I wonder whether we should be like some other families we know that completely tune that stuff out. I'm not asking you to do that, not that it wouldn't be a good idea. Just don't get too caught up in that world, okay?"

"I promise not to spend more time on Skip Skip than you do on Maniac Clown," I said with a mischievous smirk to show I meant it in good fun.

Dad smiled at that but continued as he pulled the chair from my desk and took a seat. "Yeah, but I'm thinking about more than just the internet. Everywhere you look, there are celebrities being worshipped like they have all the answers in life, when they wouldn't know how to change a light bulb in their third vacation home. And it's not just them. There are so many other people who devote their lives to this cause or that politician, and demand that everyone else either agree with them or be driven out of society.

"If you ask me, the reason so many people feel such misery and anger in the world today is because they don't have the hope that comes from faith. If there's no God and there's nothing else after this life, they wonder what there is to live for. Some people sadly decide there's no reason at all to live. Others live only for their own pleasure. Then others make a religion out of politics and these idiotic little culture fights, just blowing everything out of proportion like it's the end of the world whenever an election doesn't go their way. And if that's all there is to life, then why wouldn't it be okay to lie and hate and destroy anyone who gets in your way? They actually believe that's honorable. Broken people who say and think and do despicable things because they think the only consequence is some attention and a pat on the back from the other losers on their 'team.'

"There's nothing wrong with getting involved in politics or supporting a good, noble cause, but don't ever let those become a substitute for your faith. Your faith is your priority and anything else you want to get involved in should be based on that. So be careful about how much time you spend listening to people who want to pull you away from the truth."

"Yeah, Skip Skip rips on religion once in a while," I admitted.

"Big shock," Dad said sarcastically. "But everybody worships something, you'll notice. Everyone is born with a voice in their heads encouraging them to aspire to be something more. It's as real as our heartbeats. But a lot of people are confused by whose voice that is, and what it means to 'be more', so they look for meaning in their lives through something else. Not just the big ones like power or drugs or expensive stuff, but lesser things like popularity and followers and 'likes'. Or even a simple life of just doing whatever makes them happy, without a care in the world for anything else but their own comfort."

"Yeah, but there are people who believe in God who do that too," I countered. "Half the families of the kids in my class hardly ever even go to church."

"Oh, sure, that's totally true," Dad said. "Remember when I went to my high school reunion last year?"

I remembered. It was the only time in my life I saw my dad spend more than two minutes making sure his hair looked good, and Mom teased him about it for a month.

"You know I went to a public high school," Dad continued, "but there was a moment when I was chatting with a group of old classmates who also went to Catholic grade school with me. Sort of a 'reunion within a reunion'. Maybe eight of us sitting at a table, telling funny stories from those days. And at one point, one of the guys asked, 'Do any of you still go to church?' And the way he said it with this smirk on his face, it was like he asked, 'None of you are really that stupid anymore, right?' And a few people chuckled, maybe in agreement or maybe just to move on from the awkwardness of it, but one woman smiled and said something like, 'I don't, but that's okay. It doesn't really matter if you're still a good person.'"

"Did you say anything?" I asked.

"Yeah, I said not only did I still go to church, but that I was even a member of the men's group," Dad replied. "But I said it with a laugh, like I was in on their joke. Like saying 'Hey, isn't it funny that I'm still a weirdo?' And later I wanted to kick myself for acting that way, but the whole thing just sort of blew me away. These people grew up in religious families, went to Catholic school for 8 years, and somehow decided that going to Mass every Sunday didn't matter anymore. Worse, now they've got their own kids that they're responsible for but they're failing them in the most important job that they have as parents. They still believe in God, they're still Christians. I bet they still accept the Ten Commandments. Well, 'Keep Holy the Sabbath' is still there in print.

"So yes, lots of people want to be their own God, and lots of Catholics want to be their own pope. They ignore the truth behind the teachings that get in the way of how they want to live their lives. It's a lot easier to make their own rules. That way, nothing they do is ever wrong. Just handpick the teachings they like and if anyone tries to correct them, they pull out the ever-useful 'Hey, Jesus said not to judge others!' card. How convenient. That way, *you're* the bad Christian. As if what follows from 'Judge not' is 'so do whatever you want.' They want to determine for themselves what Jesus means by that, and 'miracle of miracles' it always happens to justify whatever they feel, and whatever they want to do."

"But it *is* wrong to judge others, isn't it?" I asked.

"Sure it is," Dad said, "but understand what that means. Only God does the judging, true, and each of us is on the path toward that moment, but it doesn't mean we shouldn't tell people when they're going in the wrong direction. Heck, we almost owe it to them, if we care about them at all. But that should be done politely and charitably. And above all, we need to focus on ourselves first."

"Is that why you didn't say more at the reunion?" I asked. "Because you're not perfect either, so you'd be a hypocrite?"

Dad shook his head with a smile. "Not a hypocrite," he said. "A hypocrite preaches a way of life that he doesn't even believe in. I believe what Christianity teaches about how to live; I just fall short many times. You know what that makes me? A sinner who needs to do better, like everyone else. You don't have to wait to be perfect before you can teach others what's right from what's wrong, but there's a time and place for that. I was wrong to practically apologize for going to church, but I don't think it would have helped for me to criticize those classmates. I might have done it for *my* glory, not God's. My pride gets the best of me. I don't mean that I think I'm holier than anyone, but too often I always have to be right. 'Sunday Mass is not optional, so if I go, I'm right and if you don't, you're wrong.' That would have been the wrong motivation for me to speak up. Usually the best way to draw people to the church is just through your actions."

"Some people's actions push people away from the church," I said, thinking of a few families who pulled their kids from my school and church in the last couple years.

Dad looked puzzled at first, then seemed to understand what I was getting at. He let out a long sigh.

"The hypocrite thing again," he said, nodding. "Lots of people say they left because of church leaders who failed and sinned, sometimes horribly. 'I can follow Christ better on my own than by being part of the Church', they'll say, even though none of that stuff has happened anywhere near our parish, thank God. And I understand the horror, and I want anyone who's hurt others to be blasted out of the priesthood and treated like any other criminal, and I'm ticked off and disgusted by the damage that has been done to people and to the Church."

Dad took another breath, having gotten himself a bit riled up. He seemed to hesitate in deciding whether to say anything more, but spoke up again after a while.

"Look, Jack, I'm not going to pretend to know what's in

anyone's heart," he said. "That's between them and God. But most of the people who left the church over this don't have any connection to people affected by that. It's okay to react emotionally, but I bet a huge chunk of people, if they're honest with themselves, would see that they only used that as an excuse. 'The church is bad and I'm too good to be one of them.' No more rules, no more Sundays spent at church, no more difficult confessions. Easy peasy. But no more Holy Communion, no more reconciliation. Did they really think through that decision? If they walked into their local church, there's a 99% chance that it's led by a good, holy priest. A church filled with good people, or at least people no more or less awful than themselves, all trying to live their faith as best they can in the Church established by Jesus himself. They're called to be there by God, and they couldn't turn away or deny that if they wanted to. And turn to what? Yourself as God? You sure can be your own God if you want. He gave you the freedom to choose. You might find pleasure and happiness, but chances are it won't end well. It's not all about you."

"But that's not the only reason people quit church," I said, thinking about the religion class that Father Drew visited. "Some people just start to doubt whether everything they were taught is really true."

"Yeah, I think just about everyone wonders that once in a while," Dad said.

"Including you?" I asked.

"Not really, not anymore," he said. "But to tell you the truth, I used to be a little afraid of hearing the other side. What if the atheists have it right? They carry themselves as these deep thinkers and scientific experts, as if Church isn't loaded with them itself. Then I heard some of the arguments. I remember

56

listening to a program where the guest's big insight was that every human is actually an atheist, since no one believes in *all* the other gods of *all* the other religions. So if everyone is an atheist, it proves there is no God. And the host, who was an atheist himself, reacted like it was the most brilliant thing he'd ever heard."

Dad looked at me like he just said the punchline of a joke I was supposed to find funny, but I just stared back at him.

"Do you see what's so ridiculous about that argument?" he asked

I thought about it for a little while before an answer came to me.

"Well, just because there are a bunch of different religions doesn't mean one of them isn't right," I said.

"Exactly!" Dad said enthusiastically. "This guy thinks that because not *everyone* knows the truth, there *is* no truth? Is the Earth not round just because some people think it's flat? That's supposed to be some genius insight? Obviously, that's not their only argument against God, but my point is that you should never let them make you feel stupid. You've got the wisdom of the most brilliant minds over hundreds of years on your side. Maybe it's enough for you to simply know that and just trust in it, but it would be worth your time to understand those arguments for yourself if you ever need to strengthen your faith."

"Why do they even care?" I asked, as Dad gave me a puzzled look. "The atheists, I mean. It's weird to me that they have, I don't know, 'thought leaders' or whatever, who make it a career to debate and write books arguing that God doesn't exist. If you don't believe in God, why do you care what others think? If nothing happens to you after you die, why waste your life worrying about what other people believe?"

"Eh, who knows?" Dad said. "Maybe they're proud like me. Maybe they find fulfillment in telling other people how smart they are and how stupid others are. Maybe they think they'd make the world a better place by eliminating religion, but that would make them moralists who are imposing their views on others, wouldn't it? How's that for hypocrisy? But I've got another theory."

He paused as if to build suspense or something, so I played my part and asked what his idea was.

"Maybe it's because they have some doubts of their own, even if they don't realize it and would never admit it," Dad said. "What if *they're* wrong? They want Christianity to be false – they need it to be – because they know they're living their lives in constant opposition. If Christianity is true, their worldview is false, and Christ is God, not them. Maybe that's why they hate it and mock us. Oh, they probably haven't given enough thought to recognize that's their motivation – a lot of them aren't big on giving much thought to anything. But if they took two seconds to reflect, they might come to realize it."

We were interrupted by a knock on the side of the doorframe, and Mom leaned in through the open door. "Everything all right?" she asked. "Dinner's ready," she said with a look toward my dad that silently seemed to add "and thanks *so much* for all your help."

"Sorry, hon," Dad said. "We're coming. I got dishes tonight." I guess he interpreted Mom's look the same way I did.

Getting up from the chair, Dad stopped for a moment before heading for the kitchen.

"Well, I really didn't plan to give a lecture," he said. "How the heck did we end up here when all I meant to do was ask you about your pal Dip Dip?"

"Skip Skip," I corrected him, as we started down the hall.

"Whatever."

6

Aw-Dumb Leaves

A few weeks went by before my next opportunity to earn service hours. Ms. Garcia had worked with the church office to send a note to all the older members of the parish, asking them if they'd like to have eighth graders rake the leaves from their yards. Once the list of homeowners was compiled, we were given the chance to claim the ones we wanted to help, and Ms. Garcia would assign any that were left over.

Figuring it would take me about two hours to rake the average yard in my neighborhood, I signed up for two homes that were not far from my own house. The Zimmermans were an elderly couple who lived a couple of blocks down the street from me. My family didn't really know them, except to see them whenever we went to the Saturday evening Mass that they routinely attended. Even when I biked past their house, it was rare to see either of them outside in their yard, which was minimally landscaped but dominated by two large maple trees that had by late October shed a thick blanket of leaves over the lawn.

Mr. Leon was a whole different situation. He lived around the corner of my block, and while I knew his last name was

Washington, he wanted to be on a first name basis with his friends – and he considered *everyone* to be his friend. Nearly every day he'd stroll down the sidewalk in front of our house during his frequent walks, once in the morning and again in the early evening. If I was outside at the time, we'd greet each other in exactly the same way. I'd say "Hi Mr. Leon, how are you doing?", and he'd respond with a loud, joyful shout, "Blessed that our good Lord has given me another day!" We might share some other small talk, but usually he'd just keep in stride, always looking sharp in a buttoned-down shirt, slacks, sport coat and a dressy cap.

At Mass, he dressed every bit as well but always added a bow tie. He sat near the back, always very deep in prayer but not in a way to draw attention to himself. Afterward, he was back to his usual energetic and happy self as he'd chat outside the church with the priests or those fellow worshippers who lingered for a while. Since he was one of the few dozen parishioners always present every Tuesday morning at our all-school Mass, I assume he attended every other weekday too.

On my better days, I'd recognize that he was the type of man I should aspire to be. My parents admired him too. I once overhead them talk about how, despite his wife having died several years before I was born, he always came across as joyful when it would be normal for people in those circumstances to struggle with their sadness. I imagine he still grieved the loss of his wife, of course, but he was close with his grown children and his grandchildren who lived in the city nearby. A person like him looked around and only saw reasons to be grateful. I looked at a ten-minute homework assignment like I'd been sentenced to prison.

So I looked forward to seeing Mr. Leon on the Saturday

morning before Halloween, which would be the following Monday. I wouldn't have to wake up too early to be able to rake both the Zimmerman's and Mr. Leon's yards before lunch. Since the leaf collection in our town was handled by workers in a truck with a giant vacuum attached to it, all I'd have to do is pull everything into a big, long pile on the lawn along the curb. That meant I not only would avoid wasting time bagging everything, but I could just show up with my dad's rake and do the whole job without ever needing to bother the homeowners.

I crawled out of bed that morning, threw on jeans and a hooded sweatshirt, crushed a bowl of cereal, and headed out into the crisp October air with a rake and a pair of gloves, looking forward to the day ahead. Once I finished the yard work, I'd come home for lunch on the couch in front of the TV with my dad to watch State U.'s football game. I had a basketball practice late in the afternoon, strategically scheduled by my sports-loving coach, who was also Mason Wallace's dad, and from there most of us would go directly to Tyler's house for a sleepover (boys don't have slumber parties). It was going to be a good day.

As planned, I was able to finish my work in the Zimmerman's yard without ever seeing them. There was a moment early on when I noticed some movement in the window, as if one of them pulled the curtain away for a quick glance to make sure there wasn't some maniac wandering around their property. By the time I looked up, there was nobody visible, but I threw up my hand in a quick wave anyway, feeling like I had to reassure them that it was just me.

There had been a decent bit of rain at the end of the week, so the leaves were wet and heavy. Even though the weather was dry that morning, it wasn't long before my shoes and socks were soaked. Still, I was glad to have the leaves sort of stick together rather than be dry and light and blowing around in the steady breeze. It made the job quicker while giving me a better workout for my upper bod. Best of both worlds.

I finished up at the Zimmerman's more or less on schedule, and made my way toward Mr. Leon's, leaving a trail of wet footprints on the sidewalk behind me. The dog walkers and joggers were out in full force, including Father Drew who was running along on the other side of the street at an impressive rate. With his focus on his pace and whatever was playing in his earbuds, he was late to notice and return the wave I gave him, so I didn't think he recognized me.

As I expected, Mr. Leon had been on the lookout for my arrival, and opened the front door as I stepped onto his lawn. Even on a Saturday morning he was dressed in slacks and a dress shirt under a lightweight dark green sweater. "Hi Mr. Leon," I said. "How are you?"

"Blessed, young Jack, I am *blessed*!" he responded with smiling eyes to match his grin.

"Good to hear," I said, returning the smile, and that was true not only for his sake but because I might have dropped dead from shock if he'd answered any other way.

"Thank you for doing me the favor of taking on this task that I am fully capable of doing myself," he said, in his characteristic slow cadence that ensured his words were clearly understood. I did a bit of a double-take, unsure if he was politely asking me to beat it. There was never a question that he was able to do his own yard work. He had two big flower beds in his front yard and a vegetable garden around the back. I didn't care about that; I just wanted to get my service hours in as easily as I could.

"And you are welcome," he continued, "for this opportunity to learn the invaluable lesson that you are commanded to serve your brothers and sisters...whether we need or deserve your help!"

The grin on his face told me I was supposed to find some humor in the way he expressed that point, while knowing he meant every word seriously. I chuckled and just lamely said, "Well, you may not *need* my help but you totally deserve it." He roared in laughter at that, though I wasn't sure why, then closed the door to let me get on with the raking. Mr. Leon had fewer leaves than the Zimmermans, but it still took me a full two hours because I wanted to make sure I did an extra good job. I was about to leave when I noticed on the front step a brown lunch bag on which was written in big, underlined letters, "Young Jack". I walked over to pick it up, and looked inside to see it was loaded with Halloween candy, presumably from the stash he'd be giving trick-or-treaters in a couple days. That guy is awesome, I said to myself, and throwing the rake over my shoulder, I took the short walk home.

* * *

The mood at basketball practice in the school gym was really upbeat. Most of us had watched State U. win its football game rather comfortably earlier that afternoon, despite being under-dogs. But mostly we were feeling pretty goofy in anticipation of the sleepover at Tyler's that night. I hadn't really spent much time at Tyler's before. Up to this point, I'd only had sleepovers with Nate or Carlos or all three of us, so hanging out as a bigger group promised to be fun, especially with the little parental supervision I expected from Tyler's folks.

Nine of the twelve boys in my class were on the basketball team. It wasn't the same nine that sat together at lunch;

Peyton's sport was hockey, and he played on a club team that traveled on most weekends. James, one of the three Roundies, made it nine. Like me, he was in the middle of the pack as far as talent went. While Tyler, Mason, and Nate were our best players, Hector, James, Carlos and I usually rotated in the last two starting positions from one game to the next. Boone never took anything seriously enough to be good at it, besides gaming, and as cool as Nic was to hang out with, hand-eye coordination just wasn't his thing.

Tyler had invited everyone to his house except Hector, who was too well-mannered for Tyler's tastes, and James. That wasn't unexpected by anyone, including them, but it still made it a little awkward at practice. We tried to avoid talking about it, in a rare display of consideration for our fellow classmates. Carlos had been invited but said he couldn't make it, for reasons he kept to himself, not that anyone asked. I didn't have to. Over the past year or so, Carlos and I had become very good friends. Nate would always be my oldest friend because our parents were so close. We were still plenty tight, but to be honest, our personalities were just starting to go off in slightly different directions, while Carlos and I were bonding more over shared interests and our sense of humor. So I knew Carlos well enough to guess that the reason he wasn't going to the sleepover was because his mom didn't want him anywhere near Tyler's family.

If Carlos was disappointed, he didn't show it at practice. We all had plenty of adrenaline but very little focus, and Coach Wallace was none too pleased. I'm sure he was looking forward to having Mason out of the house for a night, but we were only two weeks away from our first game and our brains were on another planet. He got our attention by demanding a few sprints back-and-forth across the court, and we ended up having a solid practice before it was over.

I changed into my street clothes and threw my practice stuff into my backpack next to the clean tee-shirt and shorts that I'd sleep in, a toothbrush I almost certainly wouldn't be using, and the snack bars my mom made me pack in case I got hungry.

That turned out to be a good prediction by Mom, which at the time I just figured was due to her usual uncanny ability to know what I needed before I did, like the sleeping bag I brought along only because she suggested it. The five of us followed Tyler to his place, about six blocks from school in the direction opposite from my home, and loudly marched through the attached garage and into his house. Tyler yelled "Home!" to no reply, though I could hear signs of life coming from different rooms. We rushed down a set of stairs that led to the basement rec room, where two leather couches in an L-shape faced a huge TV mounted on the wall, surrounded by a sea of carpet that we'd arrange our sleeping bags on later in the night. Along a back wall was a bar with stools lined up in a row. And on that bar - on which I'd hoped to see three or four recently-delivered pizzas - sat two bags of chips.

Tyler grabbed one and threw the other at Nic. They tore into them and passed them around while we complained about the rigorous practice, careful not to be too critical of our coach in front of Mason. A little while passed before Boone turned to Tyler. "Dude, are there any more chips or something?"

Tyler looked through the cabinets around the bar, pulled out a jar of peanuts, and stared at it briefly before replacing it on the shelf. "Let's go to Sub Station." We threw our coats back on and walked about a half mile to the sandwich shop. I wasn't the only one who didn't have any money on hand, not thinking I'd need any reason to, but a few guys ordered foot-longs that they shared with us.

It was dark by the time we started walking back to Tyler's, which added to the sense that we were finally living like the older kids we'd always wanted to be. Parading down the sidewalk between curbside rows of raked leaves and houses bedecked with Halloween decorations, we strutted along in our outside voices, obnoxious enough that a few folks peeked out their windows to learn the cause of the commotion passing by.

Tyler, in the lead, suddenly came to a stop in front of the small home next door to his. "You know who lives here? Mrs. Gunderson," he said without waiting for anyone to guess.

I remembered the name. Mrs. Gunderson was a long-time regular teacher at St. Mary's many years ago, then was an occasional substitute until she retired completely after her husband died. I bet she subbed for my class no more than ten days total, and not since we were in about fifth grade.

"Mrs. Gunderson?" said a shocked Mason. "She was the worst!" Turning to Tyler, he asked, "Remember when she called our parents after we took James' lunch bag and threw it on the roof? I got in so much trouble!" Mason and Tyler did stuff like that so often that I was surprised either one of them would remember any particular offense.

Back at Tyler's, we returned to the rec room, still seeing no sign of his parents but running into his brother Derrick, who had just finished using the basement bathroom to get himself ready for a night out. Tyler had two older brothers, Brandon and Derrick, both in high school, and both with reputations as dudes not to be messed with. "Have fun with your cuddle party, girls," he mocked, then flipped off the lights as he bounded up the stairs, laughing at his awesome prank that would have been a bit more successful if the TV wasn't still lighting up the room.

I turned to Nate, who just rolled his eyes.

After giving up on playing a card game that Mason tried to teach us, we got into a conversation about the girls in our class that soon got way more crude than I was comfortable with. I think Nate felt the same way, since he changed the subject by suggesting we watch a horror movie on the TV. Tyler pulled up a menu and picked one of those zombie movies that was more gross than scary, and by the time it ended it was about 11:30 p.m.

A few of us started toward our backpacks to grab the clothes we'd be sleeping in, until Boone said, "Gentlemen, the night is young. Let's go back out."

"What for?" I asked.

A minute went by before Tyler said, "I know." He headed up the stairs and we followed him, trailed by Boone, who was carrying two rolls of toilet paper that he grabbed from the bathroom cabinet. He flipped one to Mason.

We didn't go farther than Mrs. Gunderson's yard next door. Tyler sprinted through the row of leaves along the curb, kicking the piles further back onto her lawn. Boone threw his roll up into a bare elm tree, the toilet paper unfurling majestically in the night sky as the roll arched over a branch and bounced from limb to limb back into his waiting arms, ready for another launch. Mason was less successful, the paper staying tight to the roll and landing in the crook of a branch. He swore at the toilet paper for its disobedience, then joined Tyler in the scattering of leaves. The rest of us did too, caught up in the moment, kicking the piles around for another five minutes before a set of headlights appeared well down the street. We sprinted for Tyler's before the driver could possibly see anything, and ran back downstairs. Eventually settling into our sleeping bags, tired to the point that even Boone finally shut up, we drifted off one by one. The exhilaration of doing something mischievous had worn off for me, and my last image before falling asleep was of Mrs. Gunderson waking up in the morning to wonder what she'd done to become the target of a bunch of stupid kids.

7

Canonized

My first thought was that I was trapped in a cabin being slowly overrun by mumbling zombies. It was a combination of the dream I'd been having, whose details I was already forgetting, and the weird confusion people experience when waking up in a different place than they're used to. It took just a few seconds to remember I was in Tyler's basement, and that the mumbling came from the voices of the guys who woke up before me.

The party wasn't going to last much longer, and in fact Nate had already left. I looked at my phone to see it was a little past 8:00 a.m. The plan was for my dad to pick me up in time for us to go to straight to 9:00 a.m. Mass together. With me out of the house the night before, Mom and my sisters had planned a "girls' night" that involved evening Mass, dinner at a pizza place, and a trip to see whatever kids' movie was playing at the theater. I'd bet my life that it told the highly original story of an animated animal who learned that it was okay to be herself.

Tyler had turned the TV on to a sports program showing highlights of Saturday's college football games. If Nate or Carlos were there, we'd make fun of the people in the studio

70

trying to sound smart by using longer phrases when just a word or two would suffice. "They need to improve on the defensive side of the ball." Ah yes, the 'defensive side of the ball'. Also known as the 'defense'.

The one that drove Nate crazy was the sarcastic use of "...and oh by the way". For example, "Jimmy Bigarm is the top passer in the conference, throwing for an average of 290 yards per game...AND OH BY THE WAY, he's also rushed for 8 touchdowns this year." Wow, Jimmy's team must be playing really well on the offensive side of the ball. I swore half these guys had their brains replaced with a computer chip programmed with the same twenty lines.

But I was stuck with guys who wouldn't find the humor in that, so after changing back into my clothes and rolling up my sleeping bag, I suggested that we throw a football around on the front lawn for a little while as I waited for my dad to pick me up. We ran up the stairs, and when I caught a glimpse of Tyler's mom pouring a cup of coffee in the kitchen off to the side, it occurred to me it was the first time that I saw either of his parents that weekend. Tyler grabbed a football from a shelf in the garage, and when I followed him out onto the grass, I froze in my tracks.

I had forgotten about Mrs. Gunderson.

She was at the far end of her yard, further separated by her and Tyler's driveways, raking the leaves that had been scattered the night before. A small mound of toilet paper was piled nearby but she had only been able to pull down what she could reach with her rake. The roll from Mason's failed throw was still tightly lodged in place, and much of the paper from Boone's more successful effort waved in the wind from branches high above.

Her back was to us, but as she began to reflexively turn around at the noise we were making, I quickly looked away and ran to the end of Tyler's yard closer to hers so that I could turn my back to her. The other guys paid her no attention at all, although I thought I heard a low groan from Boone that sounded almost remorseful.

Nic changed his mind and decided to head home. He crossed the street to the sidewalk on the other side of the road rather than walk in front of Mrs. Gunderson, and the rest of us four arranged ourselves in a square before tossing the football to each other at random. I caught Boone looking over at her a few times, with a guilt-ridden expression, but she might as well have been invisible to Tyler and Mason. If my dad wasn't about to pick me up soon, I might have gone over to her and asked if I could take over the raking. But the other problem would be that the guys would have stomped me. They would have thought that my offer to help would be the same as admitting that we were responsible, as if that wasn't already obvious enough.

At the sight of my dad's car coming down the street, I threw the ball one last time to Mason, and he and the others turned to go back into the house once again. Dad pulled into the driveway and gave the guys a wave as they filed toward the house. Waiting for me as I grabbed my stuff and walked over to the car, Dad looked to his left at Mrs. Gunderson, cranked his head further to see the remnants of the original row of raked leaves, then back again to notice the toilet paper in her tree. My guts dropped into my shoes.

Dad threw the car in reverse, backed out, and parked on the street in front of Mrs. Gunderson's house before shoving the car door open and getting out. He spun around towards me, pointed at the bags in my hands, then to the hatch where he wanted me to place them, then to the lady whose raking I was about to take over. All that happened in about five seconds, and not a word was spoken.

The sound of my dad's unusual driving maneuver brought Tyler's dad to the front door. "Hiya, John," he yelled to my dad. "Everything all right?"

"Not exactly," Dad sternly replied, sharply gesturing at the mess next door.

Tyler's dad looked over, holding the door open as the other boys rushed inside. He nodded to indicate that he had also put the clues together, but just said "Boys," and closed the door behind him.

By the look on Dad's face, that launched him to another level of rage, but forcing a smile, he turned to Mrs. Gunderson and sweetly said, "Good morning, Bev. Jack would like to finish raking your yard for you. I hope you'll let him." He said that last part a little more forcefully, the hidden message being "Don't even think about letting my kid off the hook for this."

She looked over to me and barely moved her face into a joyless smile, her eyes showing a combination of sadness and disappointment. Resting the rake against the trunk of a tree so that she didn't have to interact with this little demon any more than she had to, she turned and shuffled slowly to her house.

"We'll go to the 10 a.m. Mass over at St. Pat's instead. Get to work," Dad said as I flung my backpack and sleeping bag in the back of his car. I walked over and grabbed the rake, making my way across the lawn, knowing there wasn't a chance of any of the other guys coming over to help.

It didn't take me very long to collect the leaves. Mrs. Gunderson must have barely started before we went outside, but the mess we made of her pile the night before only extended maybe ten or fifteen feet away from the curb. Dad sat in the parked car, fiddling with his phone, probably having already texted a message to my mom that we'd be later than expected. And probably telling her why. Great.

Satisfied that the yard looked better than it did even before the previous night, I carried Mrs. Gunderson's rake into her open garage and hung it on the one empty peg where she likely stored it. Walking back toward my dad, I stopped to assess her tree. If I could get up onto the lowest branch, it would be easy from there to climb higher and grab all the toilet paper. I hoisted myself up, cracking my head on a higher branch before pulling my feet onto the limb beneath me. Making my way up and around, I grabbed one roll, then the other, and dropped them to the ground below. I pulled the remaining strands, balled them up and let those fall. Knowing I wouldn't get away with even a single sheet left in the tree, I reached for the one last strip caught on a small branch above, nearly lost my footing, but was able to grab it while I carefully found a route back to the grass below. Making the four-foot jump to the ground, I gathered everything up and dumped it in the garbage can next to Mrs. Gunderson's garage.

Dad started the car as I walked toward it, and when I buckled myself into the front seat, he pulled out for St. Patrick's, the other Catholic church across town, looking straight ahead the entire time.

The silence was killing me, but I didn't dare be the one to break it. We drove a while when a low growl came from somewhere in Dad's gut. "You guys sure showed that old lady, didn't you?" he said, unimpressed. "Boys," he said, disgustedly echoing Tyler's dad. "Just cool boys being cool boys."

"Look," I started, "I just..."

"No," Dad cut me off. "Not now. Let's get our heads in the right place before we get to church."

We drove in silence the rest of the way to St. Pat's. Pulling into a parking space, Dad stopped the car and reached for his door.

"I'm sorry, Dad."

He turned to me and said, "I know you are, Jack. Now go tell God, too." Then we got out of the car and headed into church.

* * *

I expected more grief when we got home, but he and Mom didn't say much at all about it. They asked how basketball practice went, and wanted to hear whatever I cared to share about the details of the night at Tyler's. As far as the misadventure at Mrs. Gunderson's, they didn't have to ask whether it was my idea, and it seemed that my cleaning it up that morning was going to be the beginning and end of any punishment for me. It wasn't the crime of the century, after all, and they appeared to be over it. I thought about jokingly asking if I could count that as another half hour toward my service project, but even though they'd have known that I was kidding, I was more than willing to drop the topic and let their minds go elsewhere. Mom spent most of the day running errands in between shuttling Angela to and from a friends' Halloween party, while my dad did stuff around the house, stopping occasionally to watch a little football on TV. My mind and body were both a little foggy from the shortage of sleep, so I just hung around the house playing video games with Emily for a while and finishing the light load of homework that was assigned over the weekend. Through dinnertime and into the evening, family life was back

75

to normal and I went to bed grateful to have all that earlier awkwardness behind me.

The thing about having your parents upset with you, no matter how mildly or briefly, is that you really appreciate when it's over. That made waking up on a Monday much better than it usually was, but the even more important factor on my mood was that it was also Halloween.

My friends and I had already decided that we wouldn't go trick-or-treating. I went out with Nate and Carlos the year before, and we'd barely been to our fifth door before we started feeling self-conscious about being too old for it. It's hard to follow a group of adorable kids stumbling about in their elaborate costumes yelling "Twick oh' tweat!" The adults passing out candy didn't exactly gush over us, who put no more thought into our costumes than adding a mask to our usual jeans-and-a-coat attire.

I was looking forward to the day anyway. Mom still wanted to be the one escorting my sisters out around the neighborhood, but my dad was more than happy to let me take over candy distribution duty at the front door. It would be fun to be on the giving end of the disapproving stink-eye to the kids too old to be trick-or-treating. Later that night, Dad would let me stay up with him and watch some crummy horror movie. He loved those unintentionally funny, so-bad-they're-good movies. This wouldn't be a gory bloodbath, but something like "Demon Monster versus the Croco-Shark-Rantula from Outer Space."

Feeling good about life, I walked to school that morning with my sisters a fair distance ahead of me, watching Angela's wizard gown dangling from under the coat she wore over it. The fourth graders still were allowed to wear costumes to school, and to my surprise, Emily decided not to object to the injustice of it all.

Approaching the playground where students gathered before the bell rang to signal that we could go inside, the girls veered off toward their classmates. I weaved between a group of little kids playing tag, heading toward my friends, who had gathered as always along a short brick wall at the end of the parking lot. Everyone was there except Peyton.

"Hey guys," I said as I approached.

"What the heck are you doing?" Tyler asked, except he didn't say "heck". "You coming over to spy on us? See what we're doing so you can go tell the teachers?"

"What are you talking about?" I asked, truly not grasping where this was coming from.

"Just like you told on us about Gunderson, you good little boy!" he yelled.

"No, I didn't," I shot back in disbelief.

"We're not stupid, we were there," Tyler said. "Good boy, run to daddy. Tell him how holy you are, Saint Jack."

Mason and Boone laughed at that like the obedient puppies they were, while everyone else just shifted uncomfortably, looking at their shoes.

"It's my fault my dad has eyes?" I pleaded. "There was toilet paper hanging in the tree!"

Peyton arrived in time to hear that. "Whoa, I missed a good party!" he said without realizing an argument was going on. "Scored two goals in the tournament, though."

"Look out, Peyton," Tyler said. "You're not holy enough to stand next to Saint..."

For about five seconds, Tyler stood there as if time had frozen while his little pea brain searched for the most clever thing it could come up with. Hitting on something, his eyes lit up as he yelled...

"Saint Jerk! Hey everyone, watch what you do in front of Saint Jerk!"

The puppies howled with delight.

I rolled my eyes and sighed, shaking my head, and walking away. There was never any use arguing with Tyler.

Mercifully, the bell rang, and the well-trained student body all immediately ran to line up at the entrance. I kept my distance, letting the rest of my class go into the building before following along myself, considerably less excited for the day ahead than I was ten minutes earlier.

I spent the morning trying to keep my spirits up by reminding myself that there was a routine pattern to being made an outsider by Tyler to the rest of our friends. As badly as it stung at the moment, I knew it would pass after a few days, maybe a couple of weeks at most. And I tried not to take it personally. This happened to just about all of us once in a while. At the beginning of the school year, we were playing basketball outside after lunch, and when they were scrambling for a loose ball, Carlos and Tyler got their feet tangled up, tripping Tyler and sending him skidding across the blacktop. Tyler looked at his scraped knees, ran over to grab the basketball, and launched it at Carlos' waist, knocking the wind out of him. Even though it was an accident, and even though Tyler got more than even, Carlos was painted as the bad guy. Tyler walked off in a huff, and we all followed him around the rest of recess, leaving Carlos behind. It would be a few days before Tyler talked to him again, which hinted that it was okay for the rest of us cowards to do the same, and only then would Carlos be allowed to rejoin us at our lunch table.

It would be the same for me, eventually. In the meantime I

was ticked off – at Tyler for being an idiot, and at the rest of them for kissing his butt when they all knew I didn't do anything wrong.

At lunchtime, I walked up to my new and temporary best friends – Mike, Walt, and James. The Roundies.

"Okay if I sit with you?" I asked, pulling out a chair.

"Sure," Mike said, laughing. "That chair's been getting dusty since Boone got kicked to the curb last month."

I'd forgotten about that. Tyler and Mason got mad at Boone for not letting them copy his math homework one morning. Two mysteries there: how Boone developed a sudden sense of morality that encouraged him to deny the request, and why Boone of all people would be the one whose math homework anyone would want to copy.

"Not sure what you did," Mike said as I sat down and opened my lunch bag, "but thanks for the entertainment this morning, Saint Jerk."

I shot him an unamused glance.

"Just kidding," Mike quickly said. "It's no big deal. You'll make up soon, and you can go back to having lunch with the people you'd rather hang out with."

"Ouch," said Walt, pretending to be insulted.

"You guys are cool," I said.

Mike cut me off. "Jack, you can hang here as long as you want but you don't have to lie to us."

"No, seriously," I said, discovering that I meant it. "You don't treat each other like garbage. You don't treat other people that way even when they deserve it."

"Oh wow, hey guys, we invented an entirely new lifestyle," Mike said to the others. "We can call it Christianity!"

We all smiled at that, but I went on. "No, it's just that you don't have to deal with any of that drama. When we were little, I sort of felt sorry for you guys because it was like you were being left out, but it doesn't seem to keep you from...I don't know...being happy or whatever."

James stepped in. "Look, it would have been nice just to have been invited to Tyler's last weekend. I like most of you guys. But trust me – that's about the last place in the world I wanted to be. I'm guessing I didn't miss anything."

"We unlocked a great mystery of life, Jack," Mike whispered in a low but unserious conspiratorial tone. "Turns out you'll be happier if you choose to hang out with people who are decent human beings who don't make you worship them for the right to be their 'friend', or punch you in the gut if you don't laugh at the stupid jokes they make about other people, or make fun of you behind your back. And believe it or not, that's an actual choice you can make!"

"Now, can we change the topic to something important?" Walt asked. "Who watched *Captain Galactico* last night?"

8

Coffee Boy

The next day, I intentionally left for school later than normal so that I would arrive just about the time the bell rang. That way, I could go straight into my classroom instead of waiting around outside by myself and maybe having to listen to Tyler yell a few insults toward me. I ate lunch again with the Roundies and figured I'd be doing that for at least the rest of the week. As for my friends, as a group they continued to shun me and would do so until Tyler gave a signal that I was forgiven by him. But my better friends would talk to me if we were out of sight of anyone else. Already by Tuesday afternoon, Nate and Carlos caught up with me as we walked home from school.

"Hey," Nate said, in a tone that suggested he felt bad for what I was going through, even though he was partly responsible for it.

"Hey," I said back. Part of me wanted to rip into them for failing to stand up for me against Tyler the day before, but I knew I had treated Carlos the same way weeks earlier. I decided just to be grateful that they were talking with me.

"Did you get in any trouble last weekend?" I asked Nate. The

Gunderson Incident wasn't a big enough deal to trigger my mom into calling around to everyone else's parents, but since she and Nate's mom were close friends, I figured it would have been a topic of conversation by now.

"No, she knew it wasn't my idea," Nate said. "I mean, she asked me about it, I told her what happened, and she just sort of told me that it was a stupid thing to do and that she expected better out of me."

It didn't surprise me that his parents reacted about the same way as mine. Since Nate and I were our moms' first kids, they often consulted each other on their parenting decisions. We figured that out in first grade when we each got the identical punishment – no video games for a week – for putting a dead squirrel in the mailbox of one of Nate's neighbors. It was a dumb thing, but my mom was angrier that I didn't tell the truth about it. In my house, lying was the most serious crime, no matter how small. And it was one of those goofy lies that only a six year-old would come up with; I told her that the squirrel was alive when we put it in the mailbox, as if I hoped she'd have been fine with that.

"I bet no one else got in trouble either," I said. "Tyler's dad sure didn't care, and that wouldn't have been my fault anyway. He saw it on his own."

"Yeah," Nate said. "I don't think any other parents even heard anything about it."

That's what made it frustrating. Tyler or Mason could just decide to make someone an outcast for no good reason other than to show everyone that they had the power to do so. And the rest of us gave them that power by responding exactly how they wanted. Maybe there was some hope that the rest of us were starting to think for ourselves. It might be that one of the signs of growing up is that you develop enough sense to quit blindly following the popular crowd. But then again, I see enough on social media to know if that were true, the total population of adults in the entire country would only be about six.

* * *

The following Sunday I had another volunteer opportunity. The Men of St. Mary's group that my dad belonged to was serving a pancake breakfast in the school cafeteria all morning. They did a handful of those every fall and spring, raising money that they would then donate to a good cause. Most of the people we'd be serving were those who would walk over from one of the morning Masses, and since we'd gone to church the night before, my dad and I showed up in the cafeteria early enough to help finish the set-up that had already been well underway by the twenty or so men, some wives, and a few kids scurrying about.

Greeted by the smell of sausages and coffee coming from the kitchen, we walked across the cafeteria floor toward Mr. Ryan, Mike's dad, who was leading the effort and would assign us our tasks for the day. My dad and I had helped at these before, but it had been a couple years and we'd forgotten the routine.

"Good morning, fellas," Mr. Ryan said, placing a tray of silverware at the end of the table that would serve as the buffet line where diners would be served various breakfast items before finding a seat at another table. "I was glad to see you both sign up. Must be time to get Jack some service project hours, huh?" Apparently worried he had unintentionally criticized my dad, he quickly added "I mean, not that you wouldn't have come otherwise."

83

"No, that's okay," Dad replied. "It's been a while since I helped at one of these. Been meaning to get more involved."

"Yeah, great," Mr. Ryan said, seemingly unconvinced. "Appreciate the help. If you want to grab an apron from the kitchen, I can use another body on the serving line. Jack, you can help Mike finish setting cups and glasses at the tables, and then serve drinks once we get started. I think Carlos is around here too somewhere. Have fun!"

I spotted Mike walking down an aisle between tables, placing clean coffee mugs from a cart he had brought from a storage closet. Mike knew what he was doing, having worked alongside his dad at every one of these breakfasts for years, and I bet he could probably run the whole thing himself. He directed me to get a cart of drinking glasses and set those on the tables next to each coffee cup. While diners would get their plates of food at the serving line, drinks were served at the tables by volunteers coming around with pots of coffee and pitchers of milk and juice. That would be Mike's, Carlos', and my job once customers arrived.

As I mechanically walked along the tables setting one glass after another, a loud metallic crash startled me out of my semi-conscious state. Before I looked in that direction, I figured it was Carlos making his presence known. He wasn't a walking disaster, but did tend to be rather clumsy despite being a decent athlete. Sure enough, he'd dropped a metal bin of pancakes that he was carrying from the kitchen to the serving line. Fortunately, the whole thing landed right-side up with only a couple pancakes having been jolted up and out onto the floor. A man nearby set the bin into the warming tray while Carlos threw the fallen pancakes into the trash before walking over toward me as I finished placing the glasses.

"Try not to spill a pot of coffee on anyone today, okay?" I laughed.

"I think I can handle that," he said sleepily but with a smile. "Was up late playing 'Zombie Stompie'," he explained. Fair enough, I thought, although I knew his lack of sleep wasn't the main issue.

Mike called us over to the kitchen to show us where to find juice and milk in the refrigerator, and to give us a quick lesson on how to use the coffee maker. It was a giant machine that had recently been donated to the school by a parishioner, to the exquisite joy of the teachers and staff who flocked to it every morning like ants to a fallen ice cream cone. I remembered the morning it was installed, and all the teachers were late to first period because they were in the cafeteria paralyzed with awe, crowding around the coffee machine as if it was a U.F.O. that had just landed there.

It held more than enough coffee to last us through the morning, so I was relieved we wouldn't have to worry about brewing more. All there was to it, as Mike pointed out, was to put the one hose into a coffee pot, which it would fill after we pushed one of two buttons that would release either caffeinated or decaffeinated coffee. "That's very important," Mike stressed. "The orange coffee pots are for decaf. The brown ones are for regular. Take one of each with you as you walk around the floor. That's VERY important."

Yes, extraordinarily important, I thought. Nothing on the face of the planet could possibly rise to the level of importance that was inherent in the correct selection of the type of coffee poured into these pots.

It was less than twenty minutes later when I realized my sarcasm was misplaced. The first Mass of the morning had let out, and the cafeteria was buzzing with people. As is usually the case at the early Mass, the average age of attendees was, by my judgment, approximately 117 years old, and these fine people definitely believed that the distribution of coffee into their cups was a matter of EXTREME importance.

"Coffee here, please!" came the call from a table nearest the serving line. With a pot in each hand, I slowly filled their cups so as to not spill in their laps, when three people two tables over held up their cups to catch my attention and assure their rightful place in line. Emptying my pot at that table, I hustled toward the kitchen to refill, passing by several tables full of people flagging me down to make sure I came to them next.

With two full pots in my hands, I reentered the dining area like a mother bird returning to the nest with a worm, but instead of hearing anxious chirps, it was "coffee!-coffee!-coffee!-coffee!- coffee!" I scrambled to move as fast as I could, not helping but to notice Carlos slowly wandering about the tables looking for anyone interested in the pitcher of juice he had to offer. Slacker.

"Oh, here comes the coffee," said a nice older lady as I approached her and her husband. "I was wondering when you'd get to us." And although her smile and her voice couldn't have been sweeter, the underlying passive-aggressive message she delivered was "And you're lucky I don't move as fast I used to, because I was about five seconds away from HUNTING YOU DOWN, COFFEE BOY!!"

And before I would even begin to extend my arm, the decaf drinkers would loudly identify themselves as such. My mom always said she never understood the point of decaffeinated coffee, that it was like filling a gas tank with dishwater. But the decaf drinkers knew what they wanted, and recoiled at the mere thought of being given regular coffee. They'd have been less horrified if I was carrying a pot full of rat poison.

Mike had fortunately noticed the high demand for coffee and devoted himself solely to the same cause, leaving Carlos to handle requests for any other type of beverage. Before too long, but not before I found myself sweating under the hoodie I stupidly chose to wear, we gave everybody their first round of coffee. Relieved by the thought that I could take a breather, I saw to my dismay that the people were ready for their second cups. I knew there was no escape, so I took a deep breath and got myself ready for round two. I could do this. I was Coffee Boy.

Thirty minutes and about six gallons of sweat later, things calmed down. It wouldn't be much longer before a new crowd would show up when the next Mass finished, but I had a moment to catch my breath until then. Still, there was a slower but steady stream of diners arriving, so it was apparent that our breakfast attendance wasn't limited to the morning's churchgoers. Some of the adult volunteers were clearing and cleaning the tables of those who had finished eating, and Carlos was making sure each place had a clean cup and glass. I greeted two older couples as they occupied a small round table in the far corner of the cafeteria. Although they clearly were friends who had made a conscious decision to eat breakfast together, the men were in a mostly friendly disagreement about politics. It was an election year, and with the vote days away, there was no escaping the TV and online campaign ads, the yard signs, and the news stories. "Well of course we need to do something about that, but your guy's gonna make it worse, not better," one of the men informed the other.

"Henry, that's enough," a woman I assumed to be the man's wife gently scolded. "Honestly, I've had it up to my eyeballs with this election." Then noticing me and turning in my direction, she said "He can only have decaf, dear, and the same for me."

From the orange pot in my left hand, I awkwardly poured a round of decaf for everyone at the table. That nearly emptied the pot, so I walked back to the kitchen for more. Inside, Mr. Patel, the man operating the dishwasher, had caught up during the lull in the action and was chatting with the volunteer cooks. Spotting me, he grabbed a clean cup and extended it toward me. "I'll take the last of that decaf, please," he said. I filled his cup about three-quarters full before the pot ran out, then stepped toward the machine for a refill as he turned back to the conversation.

As I set one pot down to refill the other, I thought to myself that my timing was good, since the sudden increase in noise from the dining area indicated that the latest Mass had recently ended. Bracing myself for another busy period, I was about to leave the kitchen when Mr. Patel said, "Whoa! I think you had the real, high-octane coffee instead of decaf in that last pot!"

Oops. I supposed it was possible that I didn't pay close attention and hit the wrong button last time, but I had probably refilled my pots ten times in the last hour, so I forgave myself for getting it wrong once. "Sorry about that," I apologized to Mr. Patel. "Ah, no problem," he said, downing the last of his cup before walking back to the dishwasher at the sound of another tray of dirty plates being brought in. "I needed the boost!"

Back in the dining area, I saw my dad walking around with a broom and dustpan in hand, making a quick spot-check to pick up any big items that had fallen on the floor. Seeing the line starting to form, he emptied the dustpan in a garbage bin, slipped on a new pair of plastic gloves, and headed back to his station on the serving line. As he walked past me, he told me to keep up the good work, then added with a wink and a smile, "And make sure we don't have to call the cops on that table back there."

I looked in the direction he was referring to, and saw he was talking about the four people I'd mistakenly given caffeine to a little earlier. Realizing I'd have a minute before the new arrivals got through the serving line to their seats, I walked over to see if I could replace their cups with what I knew for certain was decaf in my fresh pot. As I got nearer, I could practically feel the table vibrating as if a live electric line were laying across their laps. I could see that each of their cups was empty.

"Well if you don't want kids to have a decent school, then don't vote for it! Let the ceiling crash on their heads!" one man yelled at the other, who replied even louder, "It's eighty million dollars! You can't build a school that won't collapse for less than eighty million dollars?!"

"I have more decaf," I said quietly.

"MORE decaf?!," one of the ladies hollered. "You didn't give us decaf last time. Are you sure that's decaf? I'll take decaf but only if it's decaf."

"Sorry," I meekly said. "This is decaf." Ignoring me while I filled their cups, the four went on with their two distinct conversations, a continuous stream of words at machine-gun pace.

"I must have waited thirty minutes before any employee came over to ask if they could help me and I said 'yes, you can help me' your flyer in the newspaper said this was twenty percent off but there's no tag on the shelf that says this is twenty percent off and I'm not about to head to the checkout line and be told this is regular price when your flyer says this is twenty percent off..."

"Sure you can build a school on the cheap but kids need to have technology these days it's not like when we were kids they have to teach them to use computers you can't be educated in today's world if you don't know how to use computers..."

"Their customer service is terrible you know who their manager is it's Sherry's son and he's a real chip off the old block when he was little and we went to Sherry and Ron's house one time to play cards we saw him clear as day out the window in their backyard using his little toy remote control car to chase after these poor chipmunks..."

"You could buy twenty computers for every kid in that school with eighty million dollars it has nothing to do with computers but why in the world does a school need an Olympic-sized pool for thirty kids on the swim team why not build a bowling alley while you're at it but that'd be stupid so why is a pool any different I'd gladly vote for a new school that didn't have three baseball diamonds with artificial turf is this a school or a professional sports league?!..."

I turned away from them as fast as I could, making eye contact with my dad who had a giant grin on his face. I smiled back at him, relieved that at least my mistake with the coffee didn't cause anyone at that table to have an immediate medical crisis, then quickly picked up the pace to begin serving those at the rapidly-filling tables.

The rest of the morning was busy but uneventful, not including the time I stepped on something that made me briefly wonder if someone brought their dog to the cafeteria before realizing it was only a dropped sausage. Dad and I pitched in on the overall clean-up effort even as a few diners remained to carry on conversations as they finished their coffee. The foursome whom I'd mistakenly loaded with caffeine had calmed down by the time they left, and we overheard them discuss their plans together for later in the afternoon. Dad laughed to himself as they walked out the door. "A political disagreement that didn't ruin a friendship," he said. "Actual adults. Rarer than unicorns."

Eager to watch some football, less eager to study for the next day's math test, and happy to have three more hours of service wrapped up, I hopped into the car with my dad and we headed home.

9

Hate and That Other Thing

"And now it's time for my favorite segment of the week – clapping back at the HATERS!!"

Skip Skip posted at least one new video sometime during each weekend, and it was my habit to check it out as the last thing I did every Sunday night before going to sleep. It was a good feeling to be caught up on homework and prepared for the next day's test, but the end of the weekend always put me in a slightly depressed mood. As I faced the upcoming five-day loss of freedom, Skip Skip lifted my spirits a little. Adjusting the volume on the earbuds connected to my smartphone, I rearranged myself on top of the covers of my bed and settled in.

"Today's hater," said Skip Skip, "is Will from Iowa who writes, 'Hey Skip Skip. Usually love you man, but that was some nasty stuff you said about Amber. I know you can be nicer than that. Peace.'"

I remembered the episode from the week before. The Amber he mentioned is a teenage actress who had been interviewed for an online entertainment site and talked about how much it hurt her to hear people on the internet criticize her for her looks and talent and whatever else. Skip Skip's response was to pile on even worse with a rather vicious personal attack on Amber. I'd be lying if I said I didn't laugh a few times, but it wasn't his finest moment despite being rather typical for him. But I was wondering how someone like Will who was merely making a request for kindness qualified as being a "hater."

"Thanks, Will," Skip Skip said into the camera, and held up his phone to show what was apparently a photo of Will that was pulled from the kid's own social media account. "I'll be nicer, Will. I promise I won't tell you to keep your stupid opinions to yourself, and I won't tell you that Iowa is full of nothing but stupid fools whose only friends are their cows and their sisters – but HOW CAN YOU TELL THE DIFFERENCE?! And I won't say that you look like a baby hippo that ran face-first into the back end of its daddy. THAT wouldn't be NICE!"

Belle cackled in the background while doing some goofy dance with a giant feathery scarf wrapped over her shoulders. "That's right, nothing but nice on this show!" she added, offering her usual insightful contribution.

The host continued. "But I got a serious message for the rest of Skip Nation. Be true to yourself. Don't let nobody like Will tell you how to act, how to talk, how to think," he said, unaware that he was contradicting himself by demanding exactly that from his audience. "Stand up for yourself. Forget what other people think about you. Don't ever apologize for being yourself. And remember - I love you for being who you are."

Unless you're Will from Iowa, I thought. Turning off my phone and crawling under my blanket, I wondered how many times I heard messages like that. "Love yourself." Absolutely. "Be yourself." Sure, maybe, as long as 'yourself' is a decent human. "You're perfect just the way you are." That one I wasn't so sure about. It's definitely the way people should think about their looks and their talents and things like that. Otherwise you end up being unnecessarily miserable that you can't hit a curveball or you don't look like a supermodel. But people go too far down that road and use it as an excuse for their behavior. "Yeah, I'm a total pile of donkey dung toward people I don't like, but that's just me and if you got a problem with that, get bent." Somewhere in Iowa was a kid who agreed that at least two social media influencers could be counted among the many people who weren't quite perfect just the way they were.

Still, something in Skip Skip's message about standing up for yourself stuck with me. I woke up that Monday morning determined to get back to my normal life at school regardless of what Tyler, Mason, or anyone else would think about it.

My mood as I walked to school that day was pretty foul. The weather was getting colder, and I shouldn't have stubbornly declined my mom's suggestion that I grab a hat to wear as I left the house. As my sisters trotted along a half block ahead of me, I strategized on how I would approach my classmates while trying to ignore that the wind was making my ears feel like they were being stabbed with icy needles. I figured I'd treat it like any other day. After all, these classmate grudges always tended to just fade away with ever having a distinct ending.

Six or seven of the guys, Tyler included, were huddled together but in an unusual spot nearer to the school doors where there was a break from the wind. Tyler's back was to me, so with my shoulders still shrugged up to raise my coat collar up around my face and ears, I walked around him and joined the circle in between Carlos and Hector.

"Hey St. Jerk," Tyler said. "Shouldn't you be at church today?" I caught Mason rolling his eyes and realized that even he was ready to move on. One down, one to go.

"Come on, man, get over it," I replied, hating the weak sound of my pleading voice. I found myself getting angry, and the emotion built as I thought about the ridiculousness of it all. "You know I had nothing to do with us getting caught."

"Bull!" he answered.

"No, Tyler, *you're* full of bull!" I answered, my voice rising as uncontrollably as the words coming out of me. "Either that or you're just stupid. You're ticked off at me for nothing! Because nothing happened to you! Get over it. Nothing happened to you because your mom and dad don't care what you do! They don't even care *about* you! Nothing *happened* to you because you mean *nothing* to them!"

That last part startled me, and I braced myself for the punch I knew was coming. But instead, Tyler's face went both blank and pale. Immediately I sensed the commotion of students around us, and while my first thought was that they heard everything and were coming over to watch the spectacle of a fistfight, I realized that the bell must have rung, and they were moving toward the school entrance. Looking in that direction, I saw that Ms. Garcia had opened the doors to let us inside. I was pretty sure by the look on her face that she heard at least some of what I'd said. It would be later in the day when I learned for certain that she had.

As the school day began and the morning went on, it felt to me as though things were back to normal. The guys whose desks were nearby engaged me in the usual small talk, seemingly having forgotten that I was the outcast days before. I still didn't get a read on Tyler, who sat several rows from me and spent the first class hours slouched at his desk, inattentive as usual. My bigger worry was when we rotated into Mrs. Turner's classroom

95

for science later that morning, where Tyler sat exactly one desk behind and one desk over from me. I kept my distance as everyone in the class got up to switch rooms, but once seated, I imagined that he was glaring at the back of my head the entire time, plotting his revenge.

But there wasn't any payback then, nor would there be later. At lunchtime, I confidently strode to my group's table and sat down among my friends. I felt a brief sense of shame after making eye contact with Mike at the next table but shook it off quickly. Tyler sat across and over from me, but neither he nor Mason made any objection to my joining them. I felt a little tension, perhaps just in my imagination, but everyone else carried on normally, with Boone and Peyton doing most of the talking as always. I was back in the mix, and I even noticed Tyler chuckle at a joke I made. I was pleasantly surprised, and not just because my jokes typically go over his head. Things would be frosty between us for a while, I thought, but at least we'd be able to coexist at school and at basketball practice until things got better.

Even with the late afternoon sun shining brightly, the walk home wasn't any warmer than it was in the morning. Still, the cold was more tolerable now that I had my earlier anxiety lifted from my shoulders. I walked into the house in a considerably better mood than when I left. Then I saw my mom with an expression of sad disappointment that set off an alert in my head suggesting to me that perhaps it was a good time to consider packing a bag and living in the wilderness for a few months.

"Hi," I said cautiously.

"Why don't you hang out in your room for a while until after Dad comes home," she replied, more of a command than a question.

"Ms. Garcia?"

"Yeah, she e-mailed. We'll talk later."

I continued down the hall past my sisters' room (hearing one of them ask the other, "What would be the most dramatic color for our smoke bomb?"), pulled my math book from my backpack, and started on my homework earlier than I normally would. It's sort of funny how it takes getting in trouble to force you to do the right thing. I looked at the little crucifix statue on my desk and wondered if I shouldn't be more focused on doing the right thing more often.

Over an hour later, I could hear that my dad had come home. I waited another five or ten minutes to give Mom time to update him on what Ms. Garcia shared about their little pride and joy, then walked back out past the girls' room ("We can rent a llama from the zoo!") and took a seat at the kitchen table.

Mom had her laptop out and showed me what my teacher wrote, which was a pretty accurate description of what she heard me say to Tyler that morning. Ms. Garcia also expressed in her note that although she "did not believe it to be a gross infraction of the student code of conduct," which I assumed was teacher-speak for "not a big deal," she thought it was highly out of character for me and notified my parents for that reason. It was the story of my life, a weird and unfair condition. Instead of getting more slack for being a better-than-average kid, I actually got away with less.

"So what was that all about?" asked my dad.

I told them the story of events that led up to it, how Tyler accused me of telling on him and the others about trashing Mrs. Gunderson's yard, how he led the attack on me that resulted in me being treated like a nonperson for the entire following week even though nobody's parents really cared, and how I just got sick of it and decided to say something about it.

"I stood up for myself and I told the truth," I said, and rested my case like a world-class defense lawyer.

"You said a pretty terrible thing," my mom countered. "And knowing Tyler, you're lucky he didn't give you a black eye. But even if he did, you threw a worse punch. You get that, don't you?"

"Yeah, I get it," I muttered, not really sure that was the truth. So I told Tyler that his parents didn't care about him. It wasn't anything that wasn't completely obvious to him, to me and my classmates, and to everyone else with a set of eyes, including my parents. But I suppose he didn't need to be reminded of it, especially in front of our friends. "I was mad."

"Of course you were," my dad said. "Yeah, we totally understand that. I was thirteen once too, and it stinks to get treated like that. It stinks at any age. I've got coworkers who are really hard to get along with. Mom gets yelled at by patients. It's normal to want to lash back out at them. It's human to want to scream at the world when life gets rough. And life is rough when you're in grade school and your friends abandon you for a few days, but I'm telling you now that the odds are pretty good that you're going to have much bigger problems at some point in your life. And how you respond makes all the difference in the world."

He cleared his throat and thought for a minute before continuing.

"Some of our problems in life are the result of our own decisions gone wrong, even if they were good choices at the time," he said. "But a lot more of the things that happen to us are out of our control, like what Tyler did to you. What's

98

so important to understand is that you have the choice – you have the choice – of how you will respond. I don't mean your immediate emotional reaction – whether that's sad or angry or scared – but how you'll pick yourself up. Which step you'll take next. What attitude you'll take.

"That's hardly ever easy, not when you're abandoned by your friends, or you're feeling crummy or you've been insulted or you're feeling lonely or a girlfriend dumps you. It won't get easier. A death in the family, a job loss, marriage problems, a health crisis. I don't mean you should face every problem with a grin. We're human. But lean on your faith for strength. Those are times to get even closer to God, not farther.

"Okay, I guess I got off the topic of Tyler, so the lecture's over," Dad said, leaning back in his chair. "Just know that whatever someone else thinks of you, you are loved by God. But don't ever forget that's true of the other person too."

Mom jumped in at that. Lecture's *not* over, I thought.

"And you never know all of what's going on in someone else's life," she added. "Look, I'm not making excuses for Tyler. He's old enough to know right from wrong and usually makes the wrong choice, but he's dealing with..." She suddenly stopped herself, then continued. "You just never know what's going on in someone's life."

Well I may never know, but she clearly did.

"Yeah, he doesn't have the greatest role models in his family," I said. "That doesn't make it any easier for me to...I don't know... to 'love my neighbor'," I said, referencing Jesus' commandment to his disciples.

"Oh gosh, Jack," my mom replied. "No one's asking you to *like* him, you only have to *love* him. That's so much easier."

"Huh?" I asked incredulously. "How is that easier? You can't

99

love someone if you don't like them in the first place."

"Well for starters, it's not 'in the first place'," Mom answered. "I mean, yes, everyone thinks of love as an emotion you feel after you already really, really, really like someone. But in the other sense of the word – the Christian sense – to love someone simply means to truly want the best for them, even if it costs something of yourself. That you will sacrifice or set aside your own wants and needs for the good of that person. And what that means is that love is actually an act of your will."

"I will what?" I asked, confused.

"No, your *will*," she responded with a smile. "It is your *will*. Your *decision*. It is entirely in your power to make the choice to love someone whether or not you have a positive feeling about that person. Choose to say only kind things to Tyler, or nothing at all. Choose to pray for Tyler. Goodness, no, you can't choose to *like* everyone. God doesn't ask for the impossible. But you'll find that the more you practice loving others, the easier it is to like them too."

"That goes for your wife, too," my dad chimed in.

And with that bizarre spin, so continued the lecture that I was told had ended minutes ago.

"My wife?" I asked. "Don't you have to let me start dating first?"

They both laughed at that as my dad went on with his train of thought, if that's what it was, because this track was taking me nowhere that I bought a ticket to get to.

"Well, seriously, your mom makes a really important point about what love means," he continued. "Too many people get married forgetting that love involves making sacrifices. Or more likely, they've never learned it to begin with. We grow up watching movies and shows and thinking that love is only about emotions and that's enough. You meet a cute guy or girl who makes your heart flutter. You're attracted to that person and it *feels* good. You like the way he or she makes you *feel* about yourself. And they live happily ever after as the credits roll.

"But in real life, the story goes on and if you aren't prepared to sacrifice a huge piece of yourself, then brother, you are on the road for the same disaster that more and more people find themselves in. The little annoyances build up and boil over when you each insist on doing things your way. You resent the changes to your lifestyle, the loss of some of your freedom. You start to realize how much it matters that your beliefs and values and dreams for the future weren't in sync with each other, when you thought it would be okay because of how happy you felt when you first got together. But those emotions weren't enough. They're never enough because that's not really love. Don't get me wrong, I still really, really, really like Mom. But it's the sacrifices that define love.

"And while your wife and your family should always be your priority - after God, of course - we have to keep reminding ourselves that we have to show that same love to others. To our friends and to nice people, sure, no problem, but also to those who wouldn't dream of showing you the slightest kindness in return. It might seem difficult to show love toward people who are rude to you, but that's nothing compared to the example that was set for us. You'll probably never be put in a position to have to love someone who is nailing you to a cross."

Yikes. If my words to Tyler that morning were able to land a punch, I knew where I got the skills.

"Look, I'm sorry about today," I said. "It was a one-time thing, and I just don't want you guys or Ms. Garcia to worry about me."

"You're a good kid, Jack," my mom said. "We know that. But we're saying all this now because it's an every-day-for-the-rest-of-your-life thing. Now listen. You are held to a higher standard — by Dad and me, yes, but more importantly by God - because you know the truth about him.

"Some people — maybe most people — don't know any better. Maybe they never learned anything about Christianity at all. Others who did and should know better decided to reject it because they prefer to pretend that they're in charge. Whatever the case, our job is to pray for them, to love them, and to live lives that hopefully set an example to follow, but it's not our place to judge them when we don't know all of what's going on in their lives.

"You don't have that excuse. You know better, so more is expected of you, just like I wouldn't expect Angela to be able to take your algebra test but I sure as heck expect you to nail it. I think God looks at all of us, believers and nonbelievers, in a way something close to that. And you can decide that it's unfair that more is expected from you, or you can instead decide that knowing God is the greatest gift you can possibly be given in this life, especially when you did nothing to deserve that gift more than anyone else. So when you encounter people who act rudely or even horribly, respond with love, even when that means you have to swallow your pride when every human emotion inside of you is screaming at you to sink down to that level."

"I hear you, Mom," I said, trying to absorb it all. "It's just such a hard thing to do."

"Oh, I know it is," my dad said. "It takes a lot of humility to put the needs of other people ahead of your own. You won't always succeed. God knows that I sure don't. Few of us are able to do that every single moment. We're all angels at times, and devils at others. We go back and forth, good and bad, sometimes even within minutes. Every choice we make leads us in one direction or the other. But the goal is – every day, one day after the other – to be more angel and less devil than you were the day before. More saint, less jerk."

Noticing the change in my expression, my mom asked with puzzled amusement, "What's funny about that?"

I assured them I took their message seriously, and explained as they returned the smile on my face, "It's a long story."

10

Turkeys and the Food They Serve

There probably aren't many people who enjoy Thanksgiving more than I do. I suppose it's a really crowded tie for first place with me and thousands of others, but it's hard to believe that anyone could love it *more.*

Start with the fact that it's a four-day weekend, the longest stretch of time away from school since the end of summer vacation. That's reason enough to make it worth celebrating. What puts it over the top is an enormous meal featuring the animal that happens to be the most delicious of birds in my humble opinion, a non-stop line-up of football games on television, and the official start of the Christmas season in my family.

Outside the walls of my house, Christmas began about three seconds after the last house flicked off its lights to the final trick-or-treaters on Halloween. It was a holly jolly onslaught of music on the radio and in the stores, advertisements online and on TV, and marathons of holiday movies that had been going on in the world around me for almost a month. And much like the first dusting of snow every winter, the Christmas spirit might have blanketed the area, but it was only about a centimeter deep. No noticeable increase in peace and love as far as I could tell, but plenty of invitations to celebrate the holidays with sales on electronics and coffee shop gift cards and jewelry. Lots more songs and shows about Santa and partying and landing the perfect boyfriend than about what would happen in the manger and what it means for us.

You couldn't escape it if you tried, and I didn't always want to, but inside our home it was simply autumn until Thanksgiving weekend. Only then would we decorate the house and yard, and invite the merry sights and sounds inside...but still only on a limited basis. My mom was always mindful to maintain a balance of the quiet, prayerful Advent atmosphere in the house with just enough Christmas spirit to keep me and my sisters from whining for more. She'd gradually turn up the dial as we got closer to Christmas, but the idea was to keep the family focused on anticipating the birth of Jesus. I'm not entirely sure that always worked for me, but I could admit it was nice to find some shelter from some of the songs that I'd already gotten sick of two weeks into November.

So Thanksgiving was a big day for me, which made it all the harder to face the fact that it was going to be significantly less fun this year.

There's a community center in the city near us that serves meals for people in need. They do that every evening all year round, but I guess there's a huge turnout each Thanksgiving, so the nonprofit organization that runs the place puts out a call for extra volunteers. Mr. Ryan knew a lady that works there, so he organized a few people from church to join the much bigger crew helping to prepare and serve the meal.

It was my dad's idea to sign himself and me up for a few

hours. My mom reluctantly went along with the idea. I could tell she was mostly proud of us for doing a good deed, but a little disappointed that we wouldn't be spending the day together as a family. My sisters, though, were thrilled. They would go across town to see our grandparents and cousins on my mom's side of the family for a short visit, pick up fast food on the way back, then watch one of those vomit-inducing Christmas romance movies with Mom before Dad and I got home. Gee, will the evil business man who wants to bulldoze an orphanage to make space for his evil business have a change of heart after meeting an angelic preschool teacher who shows him the error of his evil ways on Christmas Eve? What a shocking turn of events that would be! And wouldn't it be so totally perfect if the two of them actually fell in love even though they seemed at first to have nothing in common, and they adopted all fifty-seven of the adorable little children, and he carved out all of his internal organs to donate to the old folks' home, and they all lived happily ever after?

So I wasn't at all upset that I'd be missing out on that nonsense. Plus, Dad was going to record a football game for us to watch later, and Mom planned that we'd have a family celebration with a turkey dinner on Friday. It wouldn't be the ideal Thanksgiving, but all in all I had plenty to be grateful for, as I'd realize even more clearly later that day.

"Be grateful for what you have" is a suggestion I've heard all my life from my parents. They'd say that too many people complain about what they don't have without appreciating what they do. They weren't talking about needs like food and cars and houses, but things like a better car, a bigger house, and better stuff to fill it with. I can admit they had a point. I spent plenty of time wishing for different video games even though my collection is big enough that I don't even play all the ones I have.

But their gratitude message is never driven harder than it is on Thanksgiving. On that day, I always sleep in later than normal but not as long as I'd like, until the time Dad wakes me up to ask if I'm going to get ready for Mass that morning, which is a family tradition. I used to sleepily respond by asking if I *had* to, since I knew Thanksgiving wasn't one of the special non-Sunday holy days when Catholics are required to go to Mass. He'd sidestep the holy day issue and answer, "Nope, not if you don't have anything to be thankful for." That, too, was a family tradition. Needless to say, I always grudgingly and guiltily crawled out of bed.

Having learned over the years that there was no point in fighting it, I arose that Thanksgiving morning before my dad had to wake me up. After Mass with the family, we phoned my other grandparents to wish them well, and ate an early lunch before my dad and I left for the volunteer work while Mom and the girls got ready for their own trip.

Traveling on the highway for the half-hour drive to the city, I looked out on the drab landscape. While nearly all the trees had lost their leaves long ago, no snow had fallen yet. The sky was gray from one end of the horizon to the other, and few buildings had any Christmas lights shining yet in the early afternoon to add some color to the bleakness of the view outside. Since we had a few reasons to go to the city every year, the ride was familiar to me, and I looked out on the recognizable buildings and billboards while my dad hummed along to the classic rock station he typically tuned into. He wasn't any more ready for 24-hour Christmas music than my mom was.

At the polite prompting of his smartphone's directions app,

107

he pulled off the freeway on the exit toward downtown. I knew this route would take us through the State U. campus, so I craned my neck to catch a few glimpses of the top deck of the empty football stadium, which had already hosted its last home game of the season. The normally bustling sidewalks, shops, and restaurants were mostly clear of college students who had gone to their own hometowns for the holiday weekend. It all added to the dreariness I was feeling.

My dad pulled into the driveway of a parking ramp and turned toward me after choosing one of the many empty spaces. "I know you've worked with the poor a few times back home, but this might be a little different experience," he said. "In the city, people's problems often run a little deeper. I don't mean to say that our neighbors have it easier, and I don't want to paint with a broad brush, but you might see some things that are a little more...difficult...than you're used to."

Well, that's reassuring, I thought sarcastically. I must have been expressing some worry on my face, because my dad went on. "Look, you're perfectly safe. That's not what I mean. I just want you to be mentally prepared. Just do your job and treat everyone with respect and kindness, okay?"

I nodded as we exited the car, and the two of us left the parking ramp. The community center was two blocks down the street, and a line of about a hundred people had already formed outside the door that we needed to enter. As we walked past them on the sidewalk, I got a better sense of what my dad was talking about. Back home, I'd helped out a couple times at what was called a "community meal" but everyone knew without saying it that it was focused on offering a dinner to the less fortunate. Those attendees were mostly older couples and young families – a mom (and sometimes a dad) with one or more kids.

As Dad and I continued toward the entrance, what struck me about the line was that it was made up almost entirely of men of all adult ages, including a few who were muttering to themselves or an imaginary bystander, or shuffling back and forth oddly. For the most part, though, they just seemed like typical guys, some of whom appeared to know each other and were chatting good-naturedly in little groups. If not for the battered and dirty coats most of them wore, it would have looked as normal as the line outside the men's can at a sporting event.

There were a few women in line as well, each of them with a child or two sitting in a beaten-up stroller or clutching a ratty toy. I found myself finishing the walk with my head down, staring at the ground, not because I felt superior to them but because of a feeling I hadn't expected and couldn't quite identify myself...until someone else did it for me a while later.

Upon walking into the building, we were directed toward a corner of the dining hall where the volunteers had gathered to await instructions from the manager. Mr. Ryan was talking with a lady I didn't recognize, so I assumed that was his friend who worked at the center. Mike spotted me and came over to say hi, while Dad strolled toward a group of five people from St. Mary's. I guess our church didn't exactly turn out at full strength, but in total there were about 30 volunteers there to help the regular kitchen staff of the community center.

After a few minutes, a large man came over, stepped onto a stool so we could all see him, and introduced himself in a booming voice as Edward Willoughby, the managing director of the community center. "Okay folks, thanks for coming out," he said. "We're going to open the doors in about twenty minutes. I see lots of familiar faces - great to see you!" Looking in our direction, he asked, "How about you? Where are you folks from?"

Mr. Ryan's friend answered on our behalf and told Willoughby that our group was representing a church in the nearby town.

"Oh great, the Christians are here," Willoughby said with unmistakable sarcasm. "Nice of you to take one day this year to help out. I suppose you don't have any folks that need a hand in your own town."

I shot a look toward my dad in anticipation of his head exploding. Instead, his eyes had widened and his mouth was hanging open, with his head cocked at an angle as if asking himself if he really just heard what he thought he did.

In that moment, I realized that it was something like shame or embarrassment that caused me earlier to break eye contact with the people outside. I wasn't some hero that was arriving on the scene to save the day; I'd be a guy putting food that someone else bought and prepared on a plate so that some kids could have one meal before going back to the shelter they called home. So Willoughby's words cut me a little, but to heck with that guy, I thought. I showed up when I could have instead spent the day the way I wanted to.

Willoughby ignored the awkwardness he created and quickly went into his instructions. "Our diners have signed up to eat at one of two different times. We'll split you volunteers into two groups. Half of you will serve the two o'clock meal while the other half breaks bread with our diners. Then after we clean up, we'll reorganize and reverse roles for the four o'clock meal."

Our St. Mary's group would be among those serving food first, and we were assigned specific roles. Along with a couple of people I didn't know, the Ryans, my dad, and I were tasked with serving food from one of two identical food lines that were set up. As we put on aprons and gloves before heading over to man our stations, Willoughby loudly asked the entire staff if there were any final questions. One man asked who would usher out any of the two o'clock diners that might linger at their tables while we were trying to prepare for the four o'clock meal. "We deliberately have fewer people come to the second meal so that there is enough space for anyone who wishes to stay longer," Willoughby explained. "We never kick anyone out." Then in our direction, he yelled across the room, "Got that, Catholics?"

Not waiting for a response, Willoughby made his way across the hall and into the kitchen, perhaps to spread some more of his sunshine, or to sharpen a butcher knife so he could finish us off. My dad and Mr. Ryan just looked at each other in disbelief, smiling as they shook their heads.

There were six of us at the serving line, each standing behind a large warming dish. At one end near a table stacked with clean plates was Mr. Ryan serving sliced turkey. Dad was next to him on mashed potato duty. Another couple from our church served dressing and gravy, then I was serving corn. Next to me at the end of the line was Mike and his tray of green beans. Baskets of rolls and pitchers of water were on each of the tables, organized in long rows on the dining floor.

Waiting for the doors to open, I mindlessly stirred the corn kernels around in my tray. "What's the deal with the manager guy?" I asked Mike.

"I have no idea," he replied. "He wasn't running this place last Thanksgiving, so I've never seen him before. Nice guy, huh?"

"We should get back at him," I offered. "Do you know if his coat is on the rack over there? I could fill his pockets with corn.

Or maybe dump a bunch of gravy on his car."

"Sure, Jack," Mike replied. "That will definitely change his mind and leave him with very positive feelings about us all."

"I don't care what he thinks about us," I said frustratedly.

"Yeah, you care so little that you're actually considering filling his coat with corn," said Mike with a laugh. "So if you really don't care, there's no reason to let it bug you."

With that, the doors opened and the line that had formed on the sidewalk outside was now splitting in two as people made their way toward one or the other buffet table. As they shuffled down the serving line, I felt a pang of anxiety that I might say something stupid or insensitive. That worry was dispelled when I heard Mr. Ryan and my dad pleasantly greet each of the diners, with responses that were every bit as normal and polite. I'd guess that about one of every ten or fifteen men would just silently hold out his plate while staring at his shoes, presumably dealing with what I believed was appropriate to call a mental health issue. But by and large, people were mostly friendly.

My bigger problem was finding space on their plates to drop a spoonful of corn, because by the time they got to me, the plates were piled high with other items. Mike had it even worse, since most people chose to have both corn and green beans instead of just one or the other. We made it work, and no one seemed to mind if their vegetables landed on top of their scoop of potatoes.

Having gotten into a bit of a groove, a tinge of boredom set in, so I came up with a goofy game where Mike would have to mimic me when people got to our stations. So when the next person came to me, I asked "And would you care for some corn?" and Mike would also have to ask in the same tone of voice, "And would you care for some beans?"

It got increasingly entertaining – and by that I mean stupid –

as time went on. "May I interest you in some corn?" "Corn, my good sir?" "You look like a man who would enjoy some corn!" "Ding dong the corn is served!" "Wouldst thou care for a spot of corn?" "Welcome to Corn Town! Population: You!"

We were careful not to play the game with anyone who looked like they might interpret it as poking fun at them. We were just being dorks, and while we received some odd looks, most people got a mild kick out of it.

Once everyone had been served and seated, including the volunteers who would relieve us for the second meal, we had even less work to do. Dad found a washcloth to wipe up food that had spilled on and around the table, but we otherwise left things as they were for the next shift. After diners finished their meals and left the center, we'd swoop in to clear their plates and dinnerware and clean off the tables. By the time the center opened the doors to the four o'clock diners, only a couple dozen people from the first meal were still at their tables enjoying coffee and conversation.

We first-shift volunteers gathered in a group to let the new crowd enter the serving lines ahead of us. As we took our turn to load our plates, I scanned the dining room and asked my dad where our group should sit.

"Oh, actually," he said, "they want us to split up at separate tables to eat with the, um, guests." He seemed to second-guess himself and added, "But I think it's okay if you and Mike stick together." Mr. Ryan nodded in agreement and pointed out the table where he'd be eating if we needed anything.

I followed Mike through the rows of tables until he found two empty chairs next to each other. A couple of men looked up from their plates, and I offered a nervous smile. My dining companion had no such apprehension. "Hi, I'm Mike," he said with his typical cheerfulness.

To Mike's left sat a man who was quietly but messily devour-ing his dinner, his face never straying more than three inches from his plate. Across from us were three older men who clearly knew each other. Two of them were engaged in a mild argument about the election that had finally ended a couple weeks prior, while the third appeared to be acting as their referee. He looked at Mike and me with a gentle smile, and welcomed us with a gesture toward the empty chairs. "Hello boys. We'd like to thank you for sharing your time to serve this meal."

"You're very welcome," Mike said. "It's nice to be here." And he meant it sincerely.

On my right sat a younger guy who I guessed was in his early 20s. He introduced himself as Steven and thanked me for joining the table. "Maybe I'll get a break from listening about politics," he said, at which the referee smiled while the debate continued next to him.

"You've got the facts wrong!" one said to the other.

"You've *both* got the facts wrong 'cause neither of you has any *facts* at all," the referee said sternly. "You both just get the garbage you want to hear from the people who want to sell it to you. 'Click here to be told what to be outraged about today, my little puppet. We'll tell you who to hate. No need to actually think for yourself. Just trust us. We wouldn't lie to you.' Politicians. The media." Pointing at one and then the other, he added, "*You're* believing their baloney that he's your enemy, and *you're* doing the same stupid thing. They teach you not to look at each other as individuals with your own character. You're either Team A or Team B. The good guys or the bad guys. And you're buying it! Poison for sale, and you two can't get enough. Hate for sale. And it's not costing you anything but your souls. Turn that trash off and turn it around while you still can."

"Couldn't have said it better myself," Steven said, clapping in appreciation of the referee's brief speech. Turning to me, he asked "So what grade are you in?" We shared a little bit about each other, but his was the far more interesting story. He was surprisingly open about how he was staying at a men's shelter while he looked for a job. He liked rebuilding computers and started studying computer science in college for a while before leaving school for reasons he didn't explain.

"There's a ton of computer jobs out there though, right?" I asked. "At least that's what I've heard."

He smiled sort of sadly as he ate the last of the food on his plate. "Yeah, it's not hard to find job openings," he said. "But it's a lot harder to find someone willing to take a chance on you when you've made some bad mistakes in your past."

"Sorry, that wasn't any of my business," I said.

"Oh, that's all right," Steven said. "That's nobody's fault but mine." Finishing his water, he pushed his chair out to get ready to leave, then straightened his back and turned his whole body toward me. "How about this? You did some community service today, so I'll do mine by offering you some words of wisdom. You've probably been told all your life to stay away from drugs because they're bad for your health, and that's true enough. But there are a whole bunch of other walls that get put in your path if you're ever stupid enough to go down that road." Smiling, he added as he stood up, "But I don't suppose I have to tell that to a kid who spends his Thanksgiving at a soup kitchen."

"You might be surprised by how many stupid mistakes I can make," I said.

Steven found that funnier than I intended, and laughed loud

enough to turn some heads. "Fair enough!" he said. "Well then, here's a bonus word of wisdom. The only difference between your life and some of the lives around here might be nothing more than one or a few bad decisions that snowballed out of control. Keep that in mind."

"You got it, Steven," I replied. "Good luck to you, man."

"Ah, I'm gonna be okay," he said. "I'll get an opportunity soon and rebuild my life from there. It just got delayed a few years. One of the benefits of coming here is that I realize I don't have it as bad as lots of people. So many kids think their lives are horrible if they're not as popular or don't have as much stuff as others. Then there are the adults who think they're oppressed when they're not handed everything they think they deserve. I think they could all stand to spend about ten minutes in a place like this to realize how good they have it. Even I can see that. I've got plenty to be grateful for."

Throwing on his coat, he placed his hand on my shoulder for a hard but brief grab as he began walking toward the exit, saying "Happy Thanksgiving, Jack."

11

Road Rules

"Well, what did you think of that?" Dad asked as he started up the car and we buckled ourselves in for the ride home.

Not giving the question any thought, I replied "Their gravy was better than Mom's, but don't tell her I said that."

Dad laughed. "Yeah, it was a nice meal. But what I mean is, how was the experience for you? I really didn't see much of you."

As Dad pulled out of the parking ramp while I stared through the window at the darkening streets of the city, I said, "I don't know. I guess it felt good to help people. Got about four hours of service hours in. That's pretty sweet."

"Right," Dad said, pondering something in his head. "You'll have your twenty hours done, and then what? And how many hours am I supposed to get in?"

The oddness of that question got my attention. Turning to him, I asked what he meant by that.

"It's just something I've spent more time thinking about as I get older," he explained. "Am I really doing enough to be the best Catholic I can be? How can I be so committed to

God that I become the saint I'm supposed to be, when I spend most of my waking life developing project budgets and financial projections?"

It didn't seem like he was expecting an answer from me, and after a pause, he continued, "It's not that you can't be a devoted Christian even if you're not a doctor or a Sunday School teacher. But look at your mom - she spends every minute of her job helping people. She's got a really tough job, but it's such a gift to have that opportunity."

I'm not sure what look he saw on my face, but he must have felt the need to explain himself.

"I don't want you to think I have any regrets. I have a great life and a great family and I know my job is helping support you and the girls so you can go to Catholic school, so Mom can do her work part-time, so we can give to charity. All that is good. I was called to be a great husband and dad, and I think I'm doing all right there. I'd have made a lousy priest, but I sure hope you spend at least some time seriously considering that for yourself. But you can live a holy life in any job as long as you're taking advantage of every opportunity to be Christ to other people. And God knows I need to do a better job of that."

He paused for a minute as he approached the ramp to the freeway, and given his last statement, I wondered whether he was reflecting on the Westwood Incident from about a year ago. Ron Westwood was a guy who worked at the same company as my dad. One morning the two of them were in a meeting with a bunch of other people in a conference room a few floors above their own offices. The two of them set next to each other, joking around before the meeting began, and Ron mentioned to my dad that he was fighting a stomach bug, the kind that sends everything you've put into your body – and a few things that were already there – flying without warning out your back door.

The meeting got started and a short while later, Dad was having a hard time focusing because Mr. Westwood started straightening up in his chair, clearly trying to keep his door slammed shut. Dad was highly amused by this, and before long, Ron just got up and scampered out of the meeting room into the bathrooms across the hall, obvious to everyone because of the glass wall of the conference room. Everyone's eyes followed him in reaction to his sudden, unexplained departure.

Hey, I assume we've all been there, right? The problem was that the layout of the office building switched the location of the men's and women's restrooms on every other floor, and in his rush to relieve himself, Ron thundered into the ladies' room without realizing it. But everyone in the meeting saw that he'd made a tragic mistake.

The room went silent only because my dad and a few other jokers composed themselves well enough to keep from bursting with laughter. The woman leading the meeting gathered herself and tried to carry on with the agenda, until the door to the women's room opened again as a lady exited with a shocked look on her face as if she'd just escaped a slaughterhouse. Ron Westwood had stormed the compound and unleashed World War Three in one of the toilet stalls.

Ron must have realized what he'd done soon after taking his seat. I knew from my janitor experience at school that there's no mistaking the inside of a boy's bathroom for a girl's. He camped out in the ladies' room, apparently stalling for time until after the meeting adjourned so that he could avoid the walk of shame in front of his colleagues.

Dad didn't see him again until later that day. Naturally, word got around the office quickly, and when my dad went to the cafeteria for lunch, it was the topic of joking conversation among several people, most of whom weren't even at the meeting.

A minute or two later, Ron Westwood entered the cafeteria himself. In a flash of inspiration, my dad yelled across the room, "Ladies and gentlemen, let's give a cheer for 'Mr. Wrong Restroom!'"

The place went crazy with laughter and applause. Ron was clearly embarrassed by what was probably the worst moment of his career, and maybe the most awkward moment of his life, but he just raised a hand in acknowledgment and managed to force a smirk as he found a place to sit. Dad had brought down the house, and told us the whole story when he came home later that day.

He'd soon come to regret it, though. I overheard him talking about it with my mom a week or so later. "'Wrong Restroom.' It's all any of the guys at work call him anymore. I didn't mean to humiliate the guy; it was just a stupid joke. Okay, it was a pretty good joke. But I wished I'd kept my mouth shut."

Now on the highway, Dad leaned over to change the station on the radio. The news stories leading up to Thanksgiving weekend always mentioned predictions of the high number of travelers, but judging by the light traffic on the freeway, most everyone had already gotten to their destinations earlier in the day.

"So that's what I meant about counting my own service hours," Dad said. "If I'm not doing stuff like that as a core function of my job, it feels like I need to do more in my free time to help others. I guess that's true of all of us, but it just seems especially important for me."

It sounded similar to something I'd heard earlier that afternoon. "Is this about what that Edward guy said about only showing up to help once a year?" I asked.

Dad smiled and shook his head. "No, it's been on my mind for a while. But man, I couldn't believe that guy."

"I couldn't believe you didn't yell back at him," I replied.

Dad chuckled a bit. "Oh, it wasn't easy," he said. "But that's something I've been working on too. Not just acting better, but *being* better than I usually am. Trying to be less judgmental." He paused to take a minute to pull around a slow-moving van before going on.

"Here's the deal with that Willoughby guy," he said. "The man serves meals every single night to the needy. Feeding the hungry is literally his job. He doesn't seem to think much of Christians, and I don't know what he believes, but he obviously feels a moral obligation to care for those who need help. He sure isn't doing it for the money. I admire that. So what would make me think I have the right to decide I'm better than him?"

"Well, it matters that he's not a Christian, doesn't it?", I asked. "I mean, what's the point of going to church or confession or praying if all you have to do are good deeds, no matter what you think of God?"

"Yeah, you're right about that," said Dad. "The thing is that we don't really know anything about what's going on with people like that. Yes, salvation is only through Jesus, but maybe that comes later in his life, or even in the next. That's not our concern. A guy like that could spit on Jesus today and still be a million miles closer to heaven than me or you for all we know. We don't even know for sure where *we* stand with God ourselves, so how can we pretend to know that about someone else?

"But you're completely right about people needing to have a relationship with God. Loving your neighbor is great, but I have a pretty good guess that it's entirely meaningless if you don't love God. Not even *close* to good enough. God created us to know him, to love him, and to obey him. Fully and completely. Imagine if you were the greatest kid in the world outside of our house. Every teacher's favorite student, every classmate's best friend. You searched all day for stray kittens so you could house them in the pet shelters you built in your spare time, in between diapering the neighborhood kids and handing out free butterscotch candies to old folks. And then you came home, screamed the most vile curse words imaginable at Mom, swung a baseball bat to the side of my head, and shoved your sisters into the wall. That's how a lot of people treat God."

"The world's full of people who do an incredible amount to help others. That's great. But if they reject God like that? It's hard not to think that's gonna be a problem for them some day. And yet it is demanded of us that we love them, to desire what is best for them. That's not optional. So what do you do? Pray for them. Show them by example. I mean, seriously, if I had decided to chew Willoughby a new one, would that have drawn him closer to Jesus? Or make him think, 'Gosh, I was wrong about Christians – they're really super'?"

Without saying it, I understood the point. I had yet to see a yelling match that ended with one person being persuaded to the other's point of view. But my recollection of that moment spurred another memory.

"What did he mean when he was yelling to us Catholics about not kicking people out?" I asked.

"Oh yeah. Cripes, I forgot about that," he said in a tone that told me he was rolling his eyes even if I couldn't make it out in the dim light of the car. "I'm guessing he was talking about sin. Or 'rules', as he would probably put it. As in, 'the Church has too many rules on what people can and can't do and how they should live, and it's silly and outdated and mean, and the Church should really get with the times because it's the twenty-first century after all, so all these things that you say are wrong really aren't anymore, and not only do you hate people who break your dumb rules, you're all a bunch of hypocrites because you do all that and worse stuff yourselves'."

He paused, then added, "And of course that's all a bunch of garbage, except the part about us all being sinners too. Jesus said he came to save sinners, which is why the Church doesn't want to kick out sinners, it *invites* them. It *exists* for them. For *us*. But when we sin and break God's law – which is what the Church's 'rules' are, remember; they're God's law – we need to keep trying to change our lives. You can't demand that God and his church allow you to live however you want. The world isn't doing people any favors when it teaches them to yell 'Just accept me for who I am!'"

"I've got friends that say stuff like that all the time," I said, "and they're Catholic."

"Same here," said Dad. "And you've been taught the whole 'hate the sin, not the sinner' thing, and thank God for that or otherwise we'd all be moping around hating *ourselves* if we were honest about it. But it's true that there are plenty of Christians who don't take that to heart and fail to treat people kindly. Too often I'm one of them, and shame on me.

"But it might help to think about sins not as a list of made-up rules, but about things that are clearly opposed to God's purpose for us. Now I don't know if the pope or other people smarter than me would quite agree with that definition, but it works for me. And because we're created in God's image, we have to treat ourselves and other people with dignity. We can use the minds he gave us to know his purpose, right? For example, our bodies have obvious biological purposes...," and he continued as he noticed me squirm at the thought that he and I were about to relive the most awkward conversation of our lives from several months ago, "...and yeah, I'm going there, but that seems to be at the core of most of the issues that people oppose the Church on, so bear with me."

I was relieved. Hesitantly.

"And if we use our bodies in ways contrary to that purpose, we're really acting against *God's* purpose. We're sinning. That hasn't changed, and it doesn't matter if the culture has changed. The culture's a dumpster fire. The culture shrugs or even jokes about millions of people poisoning their brains with junk on the internet, then we act surprised that so many men go around treating women like dirt, like they exist just for their own pleasure. Or that some women don't see themselves as having any more dignity or value than that. It's insane."

Dad looked at the speedometer and, noticing that the speed of the car had increased at about the same rate as his voice, eased up on the accelerator.

"Anyway, like I said, that's just one example," he said, as I said a silent prayer of thanksgiving for leaving that topic. "But the point is that avoiding sin isn't about following rules as much as it is about living our lives in the way we were designed to, in the way we act with ourselves and each other. And if you don't understand why the Church considers something sinful, for goodness sake, look up the reason and you'll come to see the logic behind it. So don't buy into the lie that everything going on around you is okay, but don't ever let yourself think you're better than someone else. We all sin, and we should try not to make judgments about people who seem like jerks on the surface when we don't know their situation."

As if on cue, a gray sports car passed by in the left lane.

"Take this clown, for instance," he said, pointing toward the rear bumper of the car, on which a gold decal shone in Dad's headlights. It was the simple fish outline used as a symbol of Christianity, but with little feet as if to indicate that it was evolving out the ocean. I'd seen it on other cars before, and recognized that its message was intended to mock Christians for being stupid or something. My mom once wondered out loud why no one seemed to think it was okay to twist the symbols of any other religion, but she said it in a way that made me think she already knew the answer. I also seem to remember the word "cowards" being said under her breath.

"So this guy wants to let the world know that he's superior," Dad continued. "Never mind that he almost certainly has zero clue that the Church doesn't teach that evolution and Christianity are in conflict with each other. He just wants to rub our noses in something that he in his ignorance thinks we'll find offensive. And of course he wants the rest of the world to be assured that he's not like one of those dumb Christians. And I'm sure he gets plenty of approving looks from his fellow smug know-nothings, and probably a few middle fingers from some Christians who ought to behave better. Doesn't matter to him, though. In his little mind, either reaction just proves that he's one of the enlightened ones."

Dad paused for a few seconds before adding, "By the way, how do you think he'd feel if he caught his wife kissing his best friend?"

I was caught off guard by the abrupt change of topics, as if my dad just asked why Martians eat corn dogs on rollercoasters. "He'd be ticked off?" I guessed.

"Well, I don't see why he should," Dad replied. "They'd just be two evolved creatures following their naturally-evolved instincts, doing what their naturally-evolved brains are guiding them to do. No harm in that. In fact, a series of trillions of chemical reactions since the dawn of time led them to no other choice. Why should he feel a sense of injustice or betrayal? What does it matter that his wife broke her promise to be faithful to him? Who is he to say that's wrong? What *is* 'wrong'?"

"The moral law!" I answered.

"Huh?"

"Just something we talked about at school," I replied, hoping Dad wouldn't press me to explain it any further than I was able. Fortunately, Dad moved on.

"Now," he said, "I'm not behaving very well myself by saying these things, am I? After all, he might not have been taught well, if at all. Or he might have had a fine education, but once some questions crept into his mind and created some doubt, he never took the time to learn what the Church actually says about evolution or anything else. Maybe his only interactions with Christians were with rotten people who treated him horribly and never gave him any reason to think that the faith had anything good to offer him or the world. That happens far too often. Sometimes what turns people off about Christianity the most are self-proclaimed Christians who don't act at all like Christ.

"Here's what I do know. No matter what this guy thinks or does, no matter what happened in his life up until this moment, he is loved intensely by God. More than we can imagine, and not the tiniest bit less than you or me. So I have to swallow my own pride and choose to want what's best for him, whether or not he wants to drive around with his silly sticker. That's God's issue, not mine. Forget it and follow him."

We rode quietly for a minute while the radio played an old song from my parents' younger days that I'd heard roughly 17,000 times before. It always seemed to me that those classic rock stations played the same thirty songs over and over, so ordinary that the music was almost as unnoticeable as the sound of the engine or the heating fan.

As we pulled off the highway exit to our town, I felt like I had to break the silence just to be polite and let my dad know I'd been listening to him.

"It's hard sometimes not to feel like I'm better than people like that," I said. "I mean, I know I'm not anywhere close to being perfect, but at least I believe in God. That has to mean something."

Nodding along, Dad responded, "Oh, it means something, all right. It means there's more expected out of you. So don't compare yourself to others, like lots of people do, many Christians included. Get rid of the idea that it's enough to just give one more dollar to charity than the next guy, or to do favors for people you already like, and maybe for a few strangers you feel sorry for.

"Someone like Ed Willoughby or Sports Car Evolution Guy might not have as much expected from them since only God knows whether they know any better. They might have an experience in their lives when they're prompted to say just a single prayer, and that one action might mean more to God than all the good you've done in your entire Saints project. Compare yourself to the person *you* can be, not to people around you. We don't have any excuses because we know better. We know God is real, Jesus is real, and we know what's expected of us. 'Pray for your enemies. Lose your life if you want to save it. Take up your cross and follow me. Love one another.' Those aren't suggestions. Those aren't optional. Don't be the type of Christians who only go to church to visit the cute little baby Jesus on Christmas, then spend the rest of the year 'judging not', which they really just want to mean 'Don't judge *me*.' You can't pick the easy teachings and ignore everything else. It's a package deal."

Dad took the turn onto our street, and started wrapping up his sermon as we approached the house.

"So your burden, if you want to call it that, is that you know better. And now the choice is yours, every day in a thousand ways. Every decision, every thought, every word. It's not just about what you *do*. It's who you are and who you become. And who we *become* is really what matters. I started this whole conversation talking about whether I'm doing enough volunteer work and good deeds, and I don't mean to get hung up only on that. Our hearts and minds have to change. Yes, you have to help others, but much more importantly, you need to have a mind that's always connected to God through constant prayer. That's what really is key. Do that and every day you'll see an opportunity to serve others without even looking for it. You'll have a heart and mind that notices it and acts on it. You'll even find *joy* in it."

As we pulled into the driveway and Dad put the car in park, he must have realized it had been a pretty one-sided discussion. Turning to me, he said, "Look, there's a reason I've been talking to you more lately about these sorts of things. You're growing up and getting to the point where you'll have more freedom in your life, be more independent. I went through that too, and I made some bad choices. I want you to be a better young man than I was during those years.

"I'm responsible for your emotional and economic well-being, but I'll really only fail as your father if I don't do everything I can to help you get to heaven. The world lies to kids all the time by telling you that you can grow up to be anything you want to be. It just doesn't always turn out that way. No matter how hard you try, some things will be out of your control. But your commitment to God is up to you. 'His will be done,' and that's what will bring you peace and happiness, and yes, probably some sacrifice and suffering, but you'll be the person you were created to be."

Opening the car door, he asked, "Got it?"

"Got it, Dad," I said as I got out of the car and followed him along the path to our front door.

"Oh, and congratulations," he said, as he reached for the door.

"What for?" I asked.

Opening the door to the cheerful greeting of my mom and sisters, he smiled and said, "In only about twenty minutes, you just learned the meaning of life."

12

Palm Tuesday

"DECK the clouds, I hate this wea-ther...," sang my mom along to the tune on the radio as she slowly navigated her car through the icy, dark streets.

There wasn't as much snow on the ground as there usually was in early December. I had high hopes that we'd finally get a big enough snowfall that the guys who plow the school parking lot could create some small mountains for us to play on during the lunch break. And what we played was "King of the Hill," where all the boys climb to the top and throw each other down until only one is left standing. It could get pretty ugly, especially if someone cracked his head against a chunk of ice, but it was usually a good time.

But those days would have to wait. The temperature on that Tuesday night was just warm enough to make what could otherwise have been snow instead come down merely as rain, yet just cold enough to create some patches of ice on the road.

Mom, barely conscious of what she was saying as she gripped the wheel and focused on the road ahead, continued inserting her own lyrics into the Christmas carol. "Crud-dy crud-dy crud...poo-poop poop crud."

She was driving me to Meesler's, the town's big drugstore of the sort where only about five of its twenty aisles were dedicated to actual healthcare products. In addition to a variety of groceries, they carried some household goods, hardware, toys and games, all that stuff. They also had a couple of seasonal aisles up front that had been converted to a Christmas theme since the day after Halloween, and would probably transition to Valentine's Day even before my school's winter break ended right after New Year's.

I was on the home stretch of the Saints project, and this would be the first of two two-hour shifts that I had signed up to volunteer for. Sure, it wasn't ideal that it was a school night, but my other shift would happen during the Christmas break, and once I finished with that, my twenty hours were in the bag.

This time I was helping to raise cash for the organization that ran the local food pantry that supplied groceries to the needy, and the work was simple enough. All I had to do was stand in the area between the entrance from the parking lot and the inner doors to the store, and pass out little individually-packaged candy canes to everyone who came in to shop. If anyone wanted to give a donation, they could drop their money in the slot covering a barrel between me and a second volunteer who covered the other entrance, but no one had to contribute anything. They could just keep the candy, but I think the idea was that most people would feel obligated to give at least something that would more than cover the cost of a sugar stick worth about three cents. This whole set-up was replicated in at least ten other various stores throughout town. Pretty clever, I thought. And according to my calculations, approximately fourteen million times better than the week I'd spent mopping the boys' bathroom.

Meesler's was located in the middle of a long strip mall, with about five much smaller storefronts to each of its sides. A couple of those were vacant, but there was a laundromat, a coffee shop, a take-out Chinese restaurant, and a few retail stores, but also the drug rehab clinic where my mom volunteered each Tuesday, as she would that night. That made it convenient for her to drop me off at Meesler's, although my dad would have to pick me up at the end of my two hours because Mom's shift wouldn't have ended yet.

With the car sliding just slightly across the slick pavement as Mom applied the brakes, she let me out in front of the store before slowly driving on to park closer to the clinic. The store's outer doors opened automatically upon sensing my glorious arrival, and I was greeted by an older couple who I'd be relieving. The other volunteer who was working during my shift had already arrived, a woman about my mom's age who was standing stiffly and quietly near the second door some twenty feet away. Attempting to make an introduction, the man said to me, "You'll be here with...". Turning to the woman, he asked, "I'm sorry, miss. What was your name?"

"Danielle," she said, without looking up from the spot she was staring at on the floor.

I would normally have taken an instant dislike to her, but I was trying to do better about making quick judgments. She might have just been shy, I thought, and after all, she was spending her free time trying to do something good. She didn't come here because she was being held at gunpoint, or because she was forced to complete a school project. Still, it was going to make for a long two hours without having someone I could talk to.

The man quickly went over the simple instructions, then pointed out where I could find the boxes of mini candy canes on the floor tucked away behind the donation barrel. I was technically inside, but the semi-regular flow of incoming shoppers left conditions cold between the two sets of doors. I kept my coat on and filled its pockets with candy to hand out until I'd need to go back for more.

"It's been pretty busy in spite of the weather," the man told me as he and his wife headed outside. "Not bad enough to keep the Christmas shoppers away, I suppose."

I pitied whoever was on the receiving end of a Christmas gift from Meesler's, unless their greatest desire was a stick of deodorant or a frozen burrito. I shook off my sarcasm, recognizing that the store had plenty of holiday merchandise. In fact, from where I stood, I could see a temporary cardboard display loaded with video games under a sign that read "BUDGET STOCKING STUFFERS - $8." It looked like all of the games were a few years old but many would still work on my gaming system. While I couldn't read the titles from the distance, I was close enough to recognize the cover art for *Insanity Death Track*, an epic racing game that I played once at Boone's house. I asked my parents back then if I could have it, but they never got it for me, and I'd since forgotten about it. At a bargain price, I didn't think my parents would object to me paying for it myself, but with just a few bucks on me at the time, I made a mental note to bring some extra cash when I worked my next shift in a couple of weeks.

The sound of the doors opening drew my attention to a woman and her little girl who were entering the store. I handed a candy cane to each of them, which earned me a look of surprise from the mom.

"Oh, no, I'm sorry," she said. "I'm not carrying any cash." Turning to the girl, she said, "Honey, you need to give that back." The girl's faced dropped in disappointment.

"No, really, it's okay," I said anxiously. Feeling bad that I embarrassed the lady, whether it was by making her feel guilty for taking something for nothing or making her look like a dope in front of her kid, I added a lame "Um...Merry Christmas."

"Thanks," she said flatly as she and the girl passed through the second set of doors. Well, I was off to a great start.

It did get better from there, and the time went by quickly at first, with new customers coming into the store every minute or two. Most of the interactions went as easily as I hoped, with people noticing me as they approached the doors, understanding from their experience at other stores why I was there, and gathering a dollar or a handful of change before I even reached out with the candy. Other folks gave me the ol' "I'll catch you on my way out" line, but at least half of that group scurried out the exit many minutes later, hoping I'd forgotten whether or not they'd given anything. The last type were the 'Don't-make-eye-contact-don't-make-eye-contact-oh-for-the-love-of-all-that-is-holy-DON'T-MAKE-EYE-CONTACT!!!!' people who blew past me as if pretending not to notice me standing there holding out a candy cane. I was a little offended by those people at first, then decided to find it rather comical. I started to amuse myself by holding out the candy with my arm stretched way out toward them, and silently staring them down while slowly turning my head and body along with them as they walked by me with their eyes laser-focused straight ahead until entering the safe sanctuary of the store. Good times, although I didn't get the sense that Danielle found it as funny.

But I was sincerely most impressed with those who turned down the candy but put some money in the barrel anyway. And to my great surprise, I noticed some decent dollar amounts going into the barrel - several $5 bills and even a couple of $20s. I couldn't help but admire people who were willing to make a contribution without expecting anything in return, although I certainly wouldn't have thought less of them if they'd chosen to accept the candy canes.

Danielle was perfectly pleasant to each shopper who entered through the door nearer to her, but she maintained her silence otherwise. I entertained myself by analyzing the customers as they walked toward the store and making a mental prediction of whether they would donate. A lone teenager or a group of them? No way, I'd assume, usually correctly. But if it was just a boy who was with a girl? I guessed he'd donate to let her think what a generous guy he was. An old lady? Absolutely, unless she had an angry look about her. A rough-looking, blue-collar guy? No way. Wealthy-looking mom with a kid or two? Definitely.

It was a fascinating little sociology experiment. My predictions were wrong nearly as often as they were right, not much better than if I was just flipping a coin. Heads, you're awesome; tails, you're a tightwad. Someone who stepped out of a $50,000 luxury SUV was as apt to ignore me as someone who drove a beaten-up compact car. A young man was as likely to donate as an elderly couple. Then there were the bigger surprises. A teenage boy was pulling a dollar from his pocket, but accidentally dropped two more on the floor. He picked them up and decided to throw all three of them in the barrel. Hector's mom saw me as she came toward the store, pretended not to notice, then went out of her way to enter on Danielle's side, and blew past her without a word.

But my biggest failed prediction was of a tall, bald dude with a leather jacket on his body and a tattoo on the side of his neck. This time, I was the one avoiding eye contact to spare myself the embarrassment of even trying to hand a silly little candy cane to a guy like that. As he approached the door, I turned and bent to grab a few more candy canes from the box, stalling for the few seconds I thought it would take for him to pass by and enter the inner door to the store. After a moment, I stood and turned around, only to find him looming over me in front of the barrel.

"Good evening," he said as he thumbed through his wallet and pulled out a $5 bill.

"Hi there," I squeaked out in a startled, weak voice that was recognizable only because it sounded more like one of my little sisters'.

He dropped the money in the slot and I meekly thanked him.

"Just giving back, at least a little," he said. "Those guys were there for me when I needed them."

"Cool," I thoughtlessly replied, continuing to sound like an idiot.

"Aren't you forgetting something?" he asked sternly.

My eyes widened until I noticed him holding out his hand. I dutifully dropped a candy cane into his massive palm.

"Thanks!" he shouted, breaking into a smile as he went into the store. "It's for my old lady!"

As the evening went on, I reflected on my predictive abilities. I had a lot of work to do if I would ever be thinking about a career as a fortune teller. And I also thought back to what my dad said about judging people when you don't see the whole picture. I knew Hector's mom to be a really kind and generous lady, and my opinion shouldn't change just because she didn't drop a few coins in the barrel. Some of the others who didn't give that night – even though they looked wealthy enough – might have already given large donations in some of the other barrels around town for all I knew, and maybe had given all sorts of money and time to other charities. Those who said they'd give on their way out of the store but left without doing so might have truly forgotten, or were too embarrassed to admit they couldn't afford to part with what might seem to me like a small amount of money. Yes, it might be more likely that they were all a bunch of stiffs, but the truth was that I really couldn't know that based only on those ten-second moments in time.

I suppose the flip side of that line of thinking could work too. The teen that gave three bucks might have gone in and shoplifted a $10 bottle of vodka, but I decided only to focus on the positive.

Things slowed down considerably toward the tail end of my shift, which would come to an end at the same 9:00 p.m. time that the store closed. With half an hour remaining, a new shopper was arriving only every five or ten minutes. Danielle suggested I could go home if I wanted, since it was slow enough that she could cover both sets of doors, and she'd be the one gathering the night's donations to take to the food pantry the next day anyway. But my dad wasn't coming until 9:00 p.m., and I wanted to put in an honest two hours of work, or at least most of it. I planned to go into the store about five minutes before they closed and buy a soda to take to school the next day. Unlike the school's vending machine, Meesler's sold my favorite root beer. Oh, and *Insanity Death Track*. They had that too, but my purchase would have to wait until next time. I imagined myself spending the entire Christmas break bumping other drivers off the road before flying off a ramp that had me soaring over rivers of molten lava while demons shot flaming cannonballs at my motorcycle.

Just as I was thinking about packing things up to go shopping, a car pulled into a parking space on my side of the store. As the young woman emerged from her car, I recognized her as Nickie DeLorrio, whose family lived several doors down from mine. They belonged to our church, but since she and her brother went to the public school and were many years older than me, it's not like we ever played together as kids. In fact, Nickie babysat for us once when I was in something like second grade, so I always thought of her as the grown-up she now truly was. I knew that she had left town after graduating from high school, that she didn't marry but had a kid that was now about four years old, and that she and her daughter Grace moved back in with her parents a few months ago. I'd only seen her once since then, working as a server at a restaurant where my family had gone out for dinner. I heard my parents whisper something to each other at the time about hoping Nickie was doing all right after getting away from a "bad situation," whatever that meant, though I could guess it had something to do with the guy she'd been living with before.

As Nickie scooted into the store in an obvious hurry, I noticed that under her long coat she was wearing the bright orange pants worn by all the restaurant staff.

"Hey there, Jack," she said with a pretty and genuine smile as she stopped and unzipped her small purse without hesitation.

"How are you, Nickie?," I responded, offering her two candy canes so she could take one home to little Grace, although at that hour she was probably asleep back at her grandparents' house.

"Oh, just glad I got off work in time to make it here before the store closes," she said. "It's so nice that you're doing this."

"It's a school assignment," I quickly said, not sure why I was being defensive about it. Did I think she'd be more impressed if I thought I was too cool to be a volunteer?

"You must still be at St. Mary's, then, huh?" she asked as I nodded. "I'd have guessed you were in high school by now. Well they're obviously doing a great job with you. I'm thinking about sending Grace there for kindergarten next year, if I can manage it. Do you think that would be good for her? I just think that's so important."

Her shoulders slumped a little as she pulled out the only cash she appeared to have in her purse, two folded-up bills, a twenty and a ten. "Ugh," she sighed. "At my old job, we kept our tips every night, but now we pool them and get a check later."

She put the $20 back in her purse and prepared to part ways with the $10 bill after checking her wallet once more to see if she had a single dollar or some loose change to offer instead. "Oh well, the food pantry needs this more than I do," she said.

That wasn't entirely obvious, I thought to myself. As Nickie reached toward the donation barrel, the bill slipped out of her hand and onto the floor near my shoes.

"I got it," I said, bending down to retrieve it. Then, without any preconceived plan, no actual, conscious thought to what I was doing, I covered the $10 bill with my hand and gave the slightest squeeze.

I palmed the money. Then I straightened up and swiped my hand over the barrel to act as if I'd placed it in the slot, not needing to have a perfect technique since Nickie's attention was directed toward zipping up her purse and glancing at her watch.

"Such a gentleman!" she said, heading into the store.

I stuck my hands in my pockets, including the one with the $10 bill that I was in the process of stealing from a food pantry. In my head were two voices, a quiet one telling me to put the money in the barrel (you moron!), and a louder voice putting on a master class in rationalization, making brilliant arguments in favor of me keeping the cash. I'd spent the last few months working at service projects. Ten dollars was no big deal. That would be like me doing all that work for only 50-cents an hour. And I received way more than that in donations to the food pantry that night. If I hadn't shown up, they would have gotten nothing at all, I thought, ignoring the obvious counterpoint that they would have just found someone else to cover my shift. It was a one-sided debate, especially with visions of sugarplums and *Insanity Death Track* dancing in my head. I had an opportunity to reverse my mistake, but it was a lost cause. I was about to choose poorly.

Knowing my dad would soon arrive to pick me up, I returned the candy canes still in my pocket to the box behind the barrel, although in truth I might have kept one or four for myself. Saying goodnight to Danielle, I turned into the store as a voice on the speaker system reminded the five or so remaining shoppers that Meesler's would be closing in a few minutes, so to please bring their items to the checkout line. I grabbed a copy of the video game and continued to the refrigerated coolers to get two bottles of root beer, then made my way to the one and only checkout line still open, where Nickie was making her purchases.

As the clerk scanned some make-up and a bottle of shampoo, Nickie spotted a rack of small stuffed animals strategically placed to lure shoppers into a last-minute sale. She grabbed a pink unicorn, presumably meant to give to her daughter, and handed it to the clerk. I noticed that it was priced at $9.89.

"Your total is $27.20," said the clerk sleepily, and Nickie placed a credit card into the reader. Then she tried again...and again, as it appeared something wasn't going correctly.

"I don't know what's wrong," a frustrated Nickie told the clerk.

"Your card might not be the issue," the clerk replied. "We've had a few problems with our machines today. Sorry," said the clerk without much sympathy in her tone.

"I'll just put this back," Nickie said somewhat sadly as she returned the toy to its place on the rack and pulled out what I knew was the only $20 she had.

Now technically, I knew I'd only stolen from the food pantry, and Nickie would have been in the same situation even if I had placed her money in the donation barrel. Still, I couldn't help but feel like I was also responsible for denying a little girl her pink unicorn.

"Here, Nickie, let me get that for you," I said, holding out what had been her $10 bill.

"That's sweet, Jack," she said, "but you don't have to do that." Then her face went pale and blank as she looked at the bill in my hand. She knew. Maybe it was because the money was still folded up in the same way as when she had it in her purse, but she clearly seemed to realize what I'd done.

"But it's yours," I said frantically, trying to come up with some sort of explanation on the fly, but failing miserably. "I... uh...I couldn't it jam it in the donation slot at first, then I wanted to hurry and buy some pop before the store closed," I flailed, practically hyperventilating. "I was gonna give it to Danielle, the other lady, when I leave. But here," I said, trying again to offer the money. "It's yours."

Nickie paused for a second. "It's not mine," she said. "Not anymore. I gave it to charity. But thanks anyway." Paying for the other items with her remaining cash, she took the plastic bag handed to her by the clerk and walked out.

Watching her leave, I noticed my image in the front windows of the store, acting like a mirror against the darkness outside. I was wearing an expression I'd never seen on myself before, to match the emotions I'd never felt before. I've been embarrassed plenty of times in my life. I've felt shame and humiliation too, but this was such a deep, intense combination of all those things that I couldn't stand the sight of myself in the window.

But there I was. The kid who'd just been praised minutes before by a woman I'd deceived. A guy who volunteered for the hungry only to steal from them at Christmastime. A real great guy, I was. Saint Jerk.

"Excuse me," I told the clerk, and let the next man in line go ahead of me while I put the video game back. Finally I bought my root beer with my own two bucks, handed a confused Danielle the $10 bill as I left, and spotted my dad parked in the idling car outside.

The rain had stopped but, forgetting the need to be cautious on the slick pavement, my legs flew out from under me and I landed hard and square on my butt. How poetic.

My dad, seeing I was uninjured, although it might not have made a difference in his reaction anyway, was cracking up as I slid into the front seat. "Nice fall, Jack!" he said.

"Yeah," I responded glumly as we began the drive home. "I really blew it, didn't I?"

13

Tales from the Project

'Twas the Friday before winter break, and you'd better believe the all creatures at St. Mary's were stirring like crazy. Christmas Day wouldn't arrive until another week from the coming Sunday, but we had only about five hours left of school before we'd be free until our return in January. That reality was starting to sink in. It even finally looked like Christmas, with about a foot of snow having fallen in the previous ten days or so, though unfortunately in several smaller amounts over that time rather than as one big storm that might have forced school to be canceled for a day.

Father Drew came over for one of his occasional visits to our religion class, and I was glad for him that it was still morning. Even though we were full of eager anticipation for the vacation, there was still *some* chance of us actually paying attention to him. Poor Ms. Garcia wasn't even going to try giving us any real instruction after lunchtime, opting instead to treat us to a movie during the afternoon class periods.

But everything is relative, as my mom often says. Sure, we students were less antsy than we would be in a few hours, but compared to your average weekday morning, there was more anxious energy in our room than in a monkey cage at the zoo. Father Drew asked us to all take a few deep breaths and led us in a "Hail Mary" to calm us down a little before getting on with the class.

"First of all," he said, "congratulations on finishing your Saints in Service hours."

"YEESSSSS!!," yelled a clapping Boone, who was joined by most of us in a quick round of applause and cheers. I was a little less enthusiastic, knowing I still had one last shift at Meesler's to complete the next week, and I knew that a few others still had some service hours to wrap-up before being done entirely. Still, it felt awfully nice to be so close to finishing a project that seemed so daunting just a few months ago.

"I'm proud of you," said Father Drew after patiently waiting for us to settle down again. "Each of you went out into the community and did a great job representing our church and school; that is, if you did it the *right* way. Know what I mean?"

He was mostly met with empty stares, but even the few kids nodding back at him didn't seem to have a clue.

"Well, here's an example," Father continued. "Mason shoveled the snow around the rectory two different times in the past week. But when he finished, he didn't throw the shovel on the ground and angrily yell, 'THERE, I'm DONE! Are you HAPPY?!'"

There were a few laughs at the mental image, none louder than from Mason himself.

Father Drew went on. "And when Father Robert and I thanked him, Mason didn't say, 'Well, you're just lucky that I'm such a great guy. Aren't I just wonderful? Aren't you so lucky to know me? Me me me me ME!!"

More laughs, especially since we all knew that it wouldn't be entirely out of character for Mason if he had acted that way.

"Instead, Mason just gave us a friendly wave and said 'You're welcome,'" Father continued. "And it was freezing cold out that second day, wasn't it, Mason? You were outside for over an hour, right?"

Mason nodded modestly, an adverb I thought I'd never ascribe to that guy.

"And did you have to be there that second day?" Father asked him, seeming to already know the answer. Mason shook his head once, almost imperceptibly. "No," said Father in response, "because you told me you already finished your twenty hours. So why did you come back again?"

"I don't know," Mason said, a little embarrassed. "I just wanted to do it so that you didn't have to."

Turning to the rest of us, Father Drew said, "So, Mason did that work *joyfully*. He did it *sacrificially*, since it was physically difficult and uncomfortable, and he could have chosen to use that time for himself. And he did it even though he got nothing in return, since he was already done with his project hours. That's what I mean by doing it the right way."

Over the past week and a half, I'd been trying not to dwell on my near theft from the food pantry, but once in a while something caused me to relive the memory, like an old bruise you forget about until you bump it again. Hearing Mason Wallace, of all people, praised as a shining example of service to others put me to shame once more. Despite all the time I volunteered, despite the money landing where it was supposed to go in the end, I kept coming back to the guilt I felt when Nickie saw me with her $10.

I thought back to that night, when my dad drove me home from Meesler's and I barely said a word. I told him I was tired, which wasn't a lie at all, and I went straight to my room after getting ready for bed. As I lay down in the dark room, all I could think to do was to begin whispering, "Our Father, Who art in heaven, hallowed be Thy name..."

I never stopped saying nighttime prayers even after my parents stopped saying them with me at the foot of my bed long ago as a little boy. But I was trying to do a better job of *thinking* through the words instead of just saying them. I had decided that was an important part of becoming an adult, although I did a poor job of taking time throughout the day to pray in different ways – to take a moment to just give thanks or ask for guidance – just to be quiet and listen.

That night in bed, I continued, "Thy kingdom come, Thy will be done..."

"What IS my will?"

Now, this wasn't an audible, booming voice coming down from the heavens like God talking to Moses, and I'm not even suggesting it was God's voice at all. Just a thought that entered my mind. But whether the thought was mine or his, it was there before me, so I paused to consider the question.

"To not rip off money from single moms that was meant to feed the poor so I that could buy a video game for myself," was my immediate response, still disgusted with myself. Taking the question a little more seriously, I thought, "Your will is that I love you with all my mind, heart, and soul. And that I love my neighbor as myself. That is why you created me. It's the reason I exist. That's my instruction manual. A phone doesn't work if you try to mow the lawn or slice a ham with it, and my life doesn't work right if I use it for any other reason than what you intended. My heart will be restless, and Lord I could use some peace right now."

I remember that as I began drifting off, I asked myself, "So where do I go from here?" Again, whether it was my own thought or not, I recalled Jesus' words when he met some of his first disciples, answering my question as I fell asleep.

"Follow Me."

It was really that simple. Hard as heck to live out in everyday life, and impossible to do without constantly asking for his help, but nothing more complicated than that. Follow him.

So yes, while I had a very good understanding of what Father Drew was telling us about "doing it the right way," I knew all too well that straying from that, even for a few minutes in a drugstore on a Tuesday night, was all it took to take a giant step backward.

Father Drew walked over to an unused chair and brought it back to the front of the room. Taking a seat, he slapped his hands on his knees and said, "Now I want to hear from you guys about your experiences volunteering. What did you learn? What did it mean to you? Anyone? Don't make me call on you," he said with a smile.

Alycia Franklin raised her hand, to no one's surprise, and talked about the times she spent babysitting for her neighbor's three children without pay. That seemed to me like sort of a lazy service project, since it was her usual job to watch those kids anyway, but I guess it technically counted as volunteer work if she did it for free for a while. I'd have guessed she would have tried to do something that would get her more recognition, like curing a disease or negotiating world peace in her spare time. Father pressed her on what she got out of it, and Alycia gave a bland and possibly sincere response about how great it felt to spend time with the kids and give their parents some extra time for themselves.

And that was pretty much the same answer that all of the next few classmates provided, whether they stocked shelves at the food pantry, wrote cards to the residents of the nursing home, or did yardwork for a neighbor. "It felt good. It was rewarding. I enjoyed helping others."

After a while, no one else was eager to raise a hand, so Father started calling on people individually.

"Tyler," he said. "What was your most memorable experience?"

Tyler squirmed in his chair at the question, uncomfortable as he always was to be put on the spot during class. I had a feeling Father knew that but called on him despite that. Maybe *because* of it.

"Uh, I'm not done with my hours yet," Tyler said, hoping that would be enough to turn Father's attention elsewhere.

"Okay, but you must have already done something you can share with us," said Father, not letting him off the hook.

"Not really," Tyler stubbornly answered. "I mostly just helped the fifth-grade basketball coach during their practices. Helped the kids with drills. Cleaned up when they were done."

"Come on," Father insisted. "One thing."

Tyler started to reply, then paused for a minute, and finally asked, "Does it have to be something from my Saints hours?"

Intrigued by the question, Father raised his eyebrows slightly and said in an encouraging tone, "Nope. Not at all."

Tyler hesitated for a few seconds before talking. "Well, a couple weeks ago, I went to get some chips at the 'W', and Ollie was hanging around outside."

That didn't require any additional explanation for the rest of us, including Father Drew, now that he'd lived here several months. The 'W' was the name for a few convenience stores in town that had been around so long that I don't think anyone remembered what the 'W' stood for. And Ollie was well-known as a man of about 50 years who wandered around town, spending most of the day in one of the parks when he wasn't sitting outside a business or on a busy corner asking anyone who was nearby whether they had a dollar to spare. At the parks, he'd keep to himself, off in the distance from anyone else. My friends and I weren't quite afraid of him, but we'd all been trained as kids to leave him alone. Once in a while we'd hear that he'd been arrested for having some sort of outburst in public, but I'd never heard that he actually ever hurt anyone.

"He was asking people for money as they went in the store, but I just walked past him like everyone else," Tyler continued. "And I went inside and bought a pop and some chips, and I realized I'd have a few bucks left over that I could give to him. I never did that before so I don't know why I thought that," he added, as if answering a question no one asked.

"But then I thought I shouldn't give him cash, because they...I mean, he...might spend it on...." Tyler paused as an odd, almost sad look came over him that quickly passed. "He might spend it something not good for him. So I went to the cooler and bought one of those wrapped-up turkey sandwiches and gave it to him when I went back outside."

Father Drew started to say something before realizing Tyler wasn't finished.

"And Ollie took the sandwich and looked at me and said, 'Thank you, young man of God.'"

I think Tyler was embarrassed by saying that, so he sort of chuckled and shook his head and quickly ended his story with, "It was no big deal. Just something I remember, since you asked."

149

Father Drew dug in. "Why do you suppose that little moment stayed with you?"

"I don't know," Tyler said. It seemed as though he wanted to be done talking, but Father Drew stayed quiet until Tyler felt like he had to say something to break the silence. "No one ever called me anything like that before. I sure never thought of myself that way. But like I said, it was no big deal. All it cost me was a couple bucks, but it felt like it made a big difference to Ollie. Not just getting a crummy sandwich, but having someone show that they cared about him."

No one in the class had ever heard Tyler talk like that before, and Tyler realized it. He must have been in agony after sharing an emotion that none of us ever would have expected from him, but Peyton saved the day by changing the topic.

"I was making sandwiches for the food pantry," Peyton said, "but I cut my finger and bled all over a bunch of them and we had to throw them all away."

The boys laughed, the girls pretended to be disgusted, and Tyler was undoubtedly relieved by having the focus taken off him. The next several minutes were spent exchanging stories of similar mini-disasters that occurred during everyone's volunteer time. Anna Kemper said she was baking cookies at home to contribute to a bake sale, but preheated the oven without knowing her mom had left a plastic bowl inside. The smoke alarm went off in their house, her little brother grabbed a fire extinguisher, and when Anna opened the oven door, her brother aimed it wrong and blasted Anna in the face. She added that while there never turned out to be any actual flames, their house still smelled like burnt plastic.

I mentioned the time I goofed up and gave caffeinated coffee to those old men who nearly got into a fist fight. And I didn't know it since I didn't witness it, but Carlos said he dumped a pitcher of water on a table of diners at that same pancake breakfast.

Maria Sanchez, who helped to watch the preschoolers from 3:00pm until the last of their parents picked them up after work, shared that a kid once threw up on her favorite sweater, which she probably could have salvaged if only another boy hadn't immediately dumped his red fruit punch on her in an effort to clean up the mess. Lindsay Reese mentioned that one of the kids she tutored in second-grade math flunked his quiz the day after her first session with him. "I was com-puh-LEET-ly MOR-ti-fied!" she said with her typical dramatic flair, but was quick to add that his grades had been better since then.

Father Drew let us go on like that for a while, and although he was enjoying this unplanned story hour, it was time to regain control of the conversation.

"Good stuff," Father said with a laugh. "Even though it sounds like things didn't always go exactly as planned, you all did a lot of really great work. So how many of you think that you're a better person now because of what you did for others?"

Everyone's hand went up, even if some were raised half-heartedly. I mean, who was going to say no to that?

"Excellent," Father said. "So now you don't have any reason to ever go to church again, right?"

That raised a few eyebrows, caused some heads to snap up, and created a whole lot of confused expressions. But I thought I knew what he was up to.

"Well, you're all good people," Father continued. "You do nice things for others. That's all that matters, isn't it? Religion is just some made-up thing. God loves you, and as long as you're a good person, you don't need to go to church, right?"

Even if anyone agreed with that, no one responded since we all knew he obviously didn't believe it himself.

"Most of you are going to ask yourselves that question," Father said. "I sure hope none of you ever fool yourselves into believing it, but I bet you all know at least a few people who do. So what's the answer? What can you get from the Church that you can't get on your own?"

"The sacraments," Lindsay answered, sounding surprised that she'd come up with a pretty decent answer. "Communion and reconciliation."

"Communion," Father replied in a pretend scoff. "Why do we silly Catholics insist that's anything more than a piece of bread?"

"Because Jesus said 'This is my body'," she responded.

"Yeah, but he didn't really mean it," Father pushed back, but still acting.

"Those words are pretty clear," said Lindsay, "and then there's the other time he said something like 'unless you eat my flesh and drink my blood, you won't have life in you,' and a bunch of his followers walked away and he just let them go. He could have told them then that he didn't really mean it literally. Instead he said it again and again, so he must have meant it."

"That's right," Father said. "A lot of people forget that, or maybe they ignore it because it hurts their argument. But you're right. Those disciples walked away because they put their human emotions ahead of their trust in him." Turning to address all of us, he said, "Don't you walk away. Don't forget what you know. The Church was founded by Jesus. You want to walk away from that? You're walking away from him. The Church he established continued with those same apostles who sat at his feet to learn from him, who knew the truth and passed that faith on to us to this day. You could travel back in time and attend a liturgy that you would mostly recognize as the one you go to today. So, yeah, there are thousands of other religions that were invented just by mere men. Ours isn't. Don't buy that lie."

Father Drew sat still for a minute, although I couldn't tell if that was to allow that to sink in or just to collect his own thoughts.

"Some people have other reasons for leaving the Church," he went on. "You've heard them. What are they?"

Olivia brought up the tired argument some make that if God was real, we'd see him. I think those people can't wrap their heads around the idea that if the universe is a creation, its creator would be outside of it. You wouldn't expect to see God up in the stars any more than you'd expect to see a video game developer walking around among the characters on the screen. Okay, goes the rebuttal, but a God who really loves us would show himself to us. Well, let me tell you about this guy named Jesus.

Other classmates brought up other arguments, like how unimaginably huge the universe is, and the probability that other planets could support life. We answered these ourselves, having talked about it before. God can create what he chooses to create, and if that includes a billion other creatures on a million other planets, it really changes nothing for us.

Father was enjoying listening to the conversation, but interrupted. "Yeah, that's good, but you're talking about people who decide to no longer believe in God. What about those who still do? Why would they leave the Church?" Hearing no answers, he asked, "Bad priests?"

An uncomfortable silence settled over the room as every pair of students' eyeballs turned immediately downward to their desks.

"Yeah, let's put that out there," Father said. "Priests who have done bad things. Evil things. Church leaders who act like they don't believe a single thing they preach. And I think we're doing everything we can to put an end to that, but I understand that people are mad. I bet they're not as mad as me. Guess how many nasty looks I get when I walk around town in my collar. And I get why people want to throw their hands up in disgust and scream 'Enough! I'm out of here!'"

I heard it. I might even have heard it from an uncle and aunt. And I heard my mom say something similar to what Father Drew said next.

"But where are you going to go?" he asked. "This is still the Church established by Christ. And even when some of its members sin against him in horrifying ways, this is still the Church that holds his truth. If your math teacher went out and robbed a bank, it wouldn't change the fact that two plus two equals four. And if you discovered that a few crooks used to work at the hospital, you'd still go there when you needed surgery. I mean, you could stay home in pain and misery and not be healed, or go try to get an operation at the pizza place or the hardware store, but those places can't give you what you need. You belong to the Church you were baptized in, and it's the duty of all of us members to make it reflect the glory of God in the way we live our lives and share that truth with others."

As I amused myself by the thought of a pizza dude slicing open a patient's chest cavity with one of those pizza roller things, I noticed Father take a glance at the clock.

"Okay, I guess I've got a habit of going on too long, so let's finish up," he said, letting out his breath. "I came here to tell each of you that you did awesome with the Saints project, but my prayer for you is that this has a lasting impact on your journey as a Christian. Hang onto that. We'll talk more about this during the next semester because for many of you it's your last one at a Catholic school. Your world's going to get bigger next year. And as you might have noticed from the news or social media or anywhere else, it's a world that doesn't seem to share our values very much. Somewhere the culture decided that greedy people are still bad but envying and hating them is just super-duper, even virtuous. That there's no room for forgiveness unless you're on the same political team or the same side of every issue. That two people can do the same terrible thing, but my guy did for a perfectly noble reason while your guy should be thrown in prison. That anything – even the most ridiculous nonsense – can magically become real for whomever believes it to be so, and that you're a horrible person if you dare to point out the truth.

"Don't be a creature of the world. The world hates you, and if you think that sounds harsh, remember that Jesus said the same thing himself. Don't withdraw from the culture but don't let it change you. It's the world that needs changing, but you won't fix it all at once. Just do your best to bring light to the world in every decision you make. You can live down to the world's standards, or you can live up to God's."

With that, the bell rang to signal the end of the class period. The hallway quickly filled with sounds of students from other classrooms making their way to the cafeteria for lunch, and most of my class began to push back their chairs to do likewise before Father raised his hand to hold us in position.

"One last thing!" he sternly shouted over the noise of our chairs. As we groaned at the idea of having to wait even one more second until lunch, his expression transformed into a huge smile as he said, "Have a Merry Christmas!"

14

Reconciliation

"Santa doesn't have black hair and blue jeans, ya dingle berry!" I heard Emily shout from the kitchen.

"This one's Daddy, doofus!" Angela yelled back. "That's why I bit off his tummy to make it smaller."

Normally I had no idea what triggered these goofy conversations from my sisters, but this one made perfect sense to me. Mom had done some baking in the last few weeks but hadn't gotten around to making the traditional cut-out Christmas cookies until now, and the girls were very meticulous in using colored sugar sprinkles to decorate each one. They didn't seem to mind spending several minutes getting every detail right in their minds, and Mom was glad to spend the time together and keep them occupied during winter break.

For my part, I was busying myself by watching some television in the family room, enjoying weekday programs I never got to see on school days. My favorites were game shows and as usual these contestants were doing a fantastic job of making me feel like the smartest person on Earth. *No, William, North Dakota is not the capital of Alaska. Oh, I'm sorry, Barb, the answer we were looking for is hydrogen, not waffles.*

It was a Tuesday afternoon and to be honest, I was feeling a little bored. I'd played a few video games earlier but had a hard time getting into it since I was thinking ahead to the new game or two that I was pretty sure I'd find under the Christmas tree in only five days. My closest friends already were traveling or had other family obligations, but I don't think I'd have spent much time with them anyway. We were a little old for building snow forts and I didn't much feel like going out into the cold. I'd be doing that later in the evening when I worked my last two hours of the Saints project at Meesler's by again handing out candy to collect donations. I was looking forward to the feeling of being finished, and was counting on the fact that the other volunteer would be someone more fun to hang out with than Danielle was the last time. A true Christmas miracle would be seeing Anna Kemper or another of the cute girls from my class so I could spend two hours impressing her with my overwhelming charm. But I would later discover that my hoped-for miracle wasn't meant to be.

After my dad came home and we finished with dinner, Mom once again drove me to Meesler's on her way to volunteer at the rehab clinic.

"This is it, huh?" Mom said as we started down the road from the driveway. "The next time you volunteer for something, it'll be out of the goodness of your heart instead of for a homework assignment," she added with a smile.

"Yeah, religion class will be a lot easier after break," I responded. "And then I'll be done with it forever."

I didn't intend for that to come across as if I was excited or relieved by the idea, just noting the clear fact that it wouldn't be part of my coursework at the public high school the next year.

Mom pounced nonetheless.

"Oh, you better not ever be done learning religion," she said. "That's something you should spend time doing every day for the rest of your life. Not just praying and going to church, but reading the Bible, spiritual books, the lives of the saints. I'm still learning new and fascinating things that I didn't know even after twelve years of Catholic school. You can't keep growing as a Christian if you've only got eighth-grade-level knowledge. If you grew up to be a doctor but only knew eighth-grade biology, there'd be a pile of corpses in your operating room. And you darn well better care more about being a good Christian than about being good in whatever career you choose."

I assured her that I never felt otherwise. Besides, even though I would no longer be studying religion in school the next year, I would be taking weekly classes on weeknights in preparation for my confirmation. There was also a teen youth group at our church that did volunteer service, went on mission trips, and sometimes got together just for fun. I never would have found that interesting a few months ago but had come to realize it was something I really wanted to be part of. All my life I tagged along with my parents at volunteer jobs, but had recently started to view it as more of a duty than a reason to merely pat myself on the back and feel like a nice guy. And you could sure find a worse group of kids to hang out with during the high school years. Good grief, it was like my parents were taking over my brain.

Mom pulled alongside the entrance to Meesler's and allowed me to leave without the embarrassment of a public kiss goodbye. The one lady working the shift before me abruptly left upon seeing me, and I briefly wondered whether I too would be on my own for the next two hours. Seconds later a car that I recognized

159

pulled over near the doors, and just as I had been dropped off near the same spot, Tyler exited the vehicle and walked into the store.

I wondered whether I'd have preferred to be working both doors alone like the lady before me. It's not that Tyler and I were still fighting with each other. We sat at the same lunch table as usual and one of us would sometimes comment on what the other said. We hung out with the same group during recess and basketball practices, and would even exchange the occasional high-five during our games. But it had been weeks since we had anything close to a normal one-on-one conversation, so things still felt a little tense.

"Hey," Tyler said flatly with a quick upward nod to acknowledge me, but I'd have sworn that his eyes expressed something close to gladness upon seeing that I was there.

"Hey. Welcome to Candy Cane Land," I said dryly. He smirked politely at the dumb joke. As he grabbed some candy canes and walked over to take his place at the other door, I noticed as the car that dropped him off was pulling into a parking spot next to where my mom left her car. While Tyler was busy offering candy to a customer, I glanced past him to see a figure in a long coat emerge from the car and walk toward the strip mall. The darkness outside made it hard for me to identify which of his parents it was, and I didn't have an angle to see for certain where he or she was heading. It was either the rehab clinic or the laundromat next to it. But I knew two things: that neither of Tyler's parents worked at the clinic, and that this person wasn't carrying any laundry.

Aware that Tyler was now looking at me and seeing where my eyes were directed, I quickly shifted my gaze elsewhere, turning my head from one direction to another in the hope that he'd think I was aimlessly looking around without registering what I was seeing. To further support my charade, I quickly made some small talk with him, asking if, like me, he'd be finished with his Saints hours after this shift. Not only did that break the ice a little, but because Tyler seemed to relax a bit, I assumed he was convinced that I didn't notice anything unusual.

Customers came and went from the store in a fairly steady stream, as I might have expected this close to Christmas. As I greeted and thanked people for their donations, my thoughts kept returning to Tyler and his family. I remembered my parents telling me to be careful about judging people when you don't know their situation. An accidental glance into the parking lot brought that lesson home.

After an hour or so had passed, the flow of new shoppers died down a bit. I was thinking about walking over toward Tyler to talk some more, unsure of what topic to bring up. Instead, I had to put the idea on hold when an older man entered the door on my side. He walked in slow, long strides, with his back and shoulders straight, and his chin tilted slightly up. He wore thick glasses and a long but well-trimmed beard and was dressed in a black wool coat. He'd have looked like a bank president or the Prime Minister of Fancy-stan, except for his odd decision to wear a bright yellow ski cap with an even brighter orange pom-pom on top.

Upon seeing Tyler, me, and the donation barrel between us, the man stopped sharply and stood at attention as if he'd come upon the most unexpected sight imaginable. He looked me up and down, turned his upper body in Tyler's direction and did the same to him.

"Gentlemen," he addressed us. "Good evening. What is your purpose?"

In three long strides, he walked to a spot no more than two feet in front of me, then turned on his heel to face me directly. He was so close that I had to keep my elbow at my side as I raised the candy cane to show him my purpose.

"We're taking donations for the food pantry," I explained. "Would you like a candy cane?"

"I in fact would not," he replied crisply but not impolitely. A little stunned by that response, I lowered my hand as he took about five paces and stopped in front of the barrel. Taped to its side was a small handwritten sign that read, "Neighbor's Helping Neighbor's Food Pantry – Happy Holidays!"

He spent nearly a full minute analyzing the sign and examining the barrel, crossing his arms and bringing one hand to his chin as he contemplated his next action.

"I will in fact provide a donation to this cause," he declared, "notwithstanding the unnecessary apostrophes included in this solicitation appeal." I chuckled a bit, having long been bothered by that sign's grammar myself, as the man reached into his wallet and placed into the barrel a stiff $5 bill that looked as if it had been ironed.

He then took a few paces and positioned himself directly in front of Tyler, just as he had done with me.

"And you too are assisting in this effort," he said to Tyler, not as a question but as a statement, just in case Tyler had no idea how he found himself in the store until this man explained it to him.

"Yes sir, that's right," Tyler said weakly. I could tell he was struggling not to laugh.

"In CAHOOTS, as it were!" he added, raising his eyebrows and briefly lifting himself up onto his tiptoes. "Partners in ensuring the nutritional needs of our fellow man are met, as it were. Exceptional. And now I have purchases to make. Good day."

He began walking my way toward the inner door, then again stopped in front of me. I groaned internally, wondering what was next.

"Sir, I believe I will in fact accept your offer of candy," he said to me. I handed him a candy cane and he continued into the store, finishing with "You have my gratitude." As soon as he took a few steps inside, I turned to Tyler who was finally free to break into a laughter so deep he had to lean against the wall to keep from falling over.

"What was THAT?!," he managed to ask despite being practically out of breath.

"I have no idea," I said in equal parts amusement and disbelief. "Maybe he was a time traveler from the 1800s. Or just a visitor from the Andromeda Galaxy."

"We probably shouldn't be laughing though, right?" asked Tyler, gathering himself. "Dude might have some issues. Or he's just eccentric. But holy smokes, that was an experience!"

And it would be the last memorable experience of my entire Saints project. As was the case two weeks earlier, traffic into the store slowed considerably as it approached closing time. The tension broken by the strange encounter with Old Man Yellow Cap, Tyler and I spent the rest of the shift talking about vacation, school, and basketball, and even though we had never been best of friends, it was a relief to truly connect again.

A few minutes before 9:00 p.m., I asked Tyler to cover for me so I could do some quick shopping. I headed inside toward the bin of video games...and reluctantly kept walking. Even though I brought more than enough money to cover the cost of *Insanity Death Track*, I earlier made the decision to deny myself the game as sort of a small act of penance. It really wasn't that big of a sacrifice, figuring I'd probably get some newer video games for Christmas, but it felt like the right move anyway.

I went to the greeting card aisle and found one appropriate for the occasion, then remembered to get a gift bag. I took those to the checkout aisle that had the stuffed animals, grabbed the pink unicorn, and made my purchases. I asked the clerk to lend me a pen and wrote on the card as she continued helping customers. Handing the pen back to her, I went out into the doorway to find Tyler helping a lady from the food pantry who stopped by to collect the day's donations. Feeling generous, I gave her the change from my purchase and went out to the parking lot where my dad was waiting for me, noticing Tyler's parents' car also idling in front of Meesler's, ready to pick him up.

"Thanks, Jack, you didn't have to buy me anything," said my dad as I climbed into the car with the present.

"You won't be surprised to learn it's not for you," I said, pointing to the princesses and fairies pictured on the pink gift bag. "Can we stop in front of DeLorrio's house so I can drop this off quick?"

"Ooh, someone's got a crush!," Dad said before quickly adding, "Wait, one of them's too old for you and the other one's way too young."

"It's nothing like that," I replied. "Just let your son do something nice, okay?"

Dad took the cue and left it at that. We talked about how things went at the store, as Dad adjusted the route home to take us past DeLorrio's. I didn't want to interrupt the family, so I ran around to a side door that led from their house to the driveway. It was a clear night so I didn't have to worry that the present might get buried in snow before the morning. Plus, I didn't see Nickie's car, so she would find it as soon as she got home from work or wherever she was. I left the gift bag on the step, placed the card inside, and ran back to the car to complete the ride home.

* * *

"Merry Skip-mas to my NATIOOOONNN!!!"

So began the holiday edition of Skip Skip's latest video, which I started to watch before going to bed that night. I was feeling pretty good about myself. Not only did I have all my service hours done, but I think I had finally erased my guilt about Nickie and her $10. It felt like my problems with Tyler were in past and we were back to the way things were, at least until the next time he decided to get ticked off at me. But I wasn't so sure there'd be a next time in the near future. Best of all, winter break was only a few days old and it still wasn't even Christmas yet. I thought I earned a little Skip Skip time to top off what had been a rather excellent night.

"It's the holiday season, Nation, and Santa Skip's got all sorts of presents for you good boys and girls," he yelled, wearing a Santa coat over his shirtless torso, with a matching hat crammed over his mop of blond hair. "And I even got somethin' special for the *bad* girls too!"

Belle was dancing around behind him waving a long strand of tinsel in the air, engaged in some kind of idiotic gymnastics routine. In fake disgust at what he'd said, she wrapped the tinsel around his neck in a pretend effort to strangle him with it. He gleefully fought her off and she went back to leaping around in the background.

"Okay, okay," he continued with a laugh as he regathered himself. "We'll talk about that later, ladies! But right now we've got to celebrate the best time of the year! It's time to party with your friends! It's time to get together with your family...if you like any of them!"

Belle chimed in at that, having picked up a potted plant and holding it over her head as if it was mistletoe, while making kissing faces at the camera. "But EVERYBODY loves YOU, Skip!"

"Not all of 'em," he said. "Not Aunt and Uncle Too-Good who don't APPROVE of my lifestyle. I'm too *real* for them. That's okay, they'll be in church anyway. Won't have to worry about seeing ME there!"

Skip Skip took off his Santa hat and placed it over his heart as he looked seriously into the camera.

"And that gets us to the real reason we celebrate," he said solemnly, then widened his eyes with a grin as he yelled, "That cute little baby boy whose mama got in trouble thousands of years ago!"

"SKIP!" yelled Belle as she threw her head back in laughter. "OMG!"

I kept watching, a bit stunned and unsure of what I just heard.

"Oh, it's okay," Skip continued. "It was a MIRACLE, right?! I'm gonna try that next time my girl finds another woman's clothes in my apartment. That's not my dress...it's the Holy Spirit's!!!"

I stopped the video and lay there on my bed for a minute, angry enough to feel my heart pounding in my chest. I was used to the guy being obnoxious, and maybe it was just the first time I felt directly offended by him, but that was crossing the line. It was a pretty typical attitude, though, I thought. I mean, even people who wouldn't ever think to be disrespectful still didn't seem to treat Christmas as anything more than a time to have nice visits with family, to go to work parties, to maybe try to not be a complete donkey to strangers for a few days. All well and good, but the creator of the universe becoming human? A shot at redemption for us lousy people? Peace on Earth? Seems like all that ought to matter a little.

Against my better judgment, and more out of habit than anything, I checked the comments that were posted under Skip Skip's video. I should have known better. If Skip Skip's words were a 9 on a 1-10 scale of vile dog vomit, his followers were looking to push the top of the scale to 100. I found myself reacting as if these people were insulting my own mother and came to realize they actually were, just not the one who was still working at the rehab clinic that night.

Oddly, it was one of the tamer responses that set me off the most.

"Oh you dun did it skip," typed the eloquent, grammar-challenged follower 'Frankenslime6006'. "Da Jesus freaks comin for ya but no 1s more BRAVE then u King!!"

I kept staring back at one word in its ALL-CAPS idiocy. "BRAVE."

Horse crap.

What a hot, stinking mountain of pure-grade, fly-ridden horse crap. Brave? Skip Skip was *brave*?! He had thousands of half-witted, imbecilic screech monkeys howling in delight and clapping like stupid little wind-up toys, and any Christian who dared to stand up to it would get shouted down by the same mob of brainless, heartless clods. And he knew it. He *knew* he'd get praised, not criticized. Even more important to him was the *attention* he probably expected, which is all that seems to matter to people like him anyway. He was famous enough that a little 'controversy' might even get him interviewed by some bubbleheaded journalist who would pounce all over anyone who dared suggest that some remote tribe in a distant land might have some obviously goofy religious beliefs or rituals, but wouldn't ever *dream* of asking Skip Skip if he should consider apologizing about this. No, indeed. He chose the right target to crap all over. The safe target. Ooooh, how '*edgy.*' No apology necessary, oh Brave Celebrity. We'll all keep praising you, buying your stuff, making you rich. Cowards.

Brave, I disgustedly thought to myself. Want to be brave? Want to be a rebel? Be different from everyone else in the world? Stand up for God publicly and without fear when the moment calls for it. Not only be a Christian, but act like one, not just throwing a cross around your neck and self-righteously proclaiming that God's clearly on your team so anyone who thinks differently than you and your activist cause is a monster who deserves to be punished. It means praying for and loving the same people that hate you for who you are, and *good Lord, that's so hard to do*, I thought as I lay in bed trying to calm myself down. *Love is an act of the will*, I heard from the blended voice of my parents, teachers, and priests in my mind. A heroic act. A heroic choice, but one God himself demands that we make.

I thought about Skip Skip's choices. The guy had legions of followers listening to him week after week, and *that* was what he chose to say? And what about *my* choices? Like everyone else, I had hundreds every day, and each little decision formed me in some way. We choose what to listen to and what to read. We choose our friends and decide whether to lead them toward our values or follow their behavior instead. We choose whether to seek God's approval or the world's. You'd rather have the *world's* approval? Why? Seriously, why?

I flipped on the lamp above my bed so I could better see what I was doing, which was to temporarily disobey my dad, but I didn't think he'd mind if he ever found out.

I quickly created an account on the platform that hosted Skip Skip's video so I could leave a comment of my own, and smiled as I decided on a user name. I said a quick prayer asking forgiveness for the awful things I just thought about him and about his followers, and considered the appropriate words for my note. I typed a short message, hit 'submit', and checked to make sure it was entered with all the other comments. It read:

"**Saint Jerk says**: You had a choice to make the world a better place today. You failed miserably and the world's a darker place because of your decision. But God still loves you and you'll get lots more chances. It's not too late...until it's too late."

I shrugged my shoulders, realizing it wasn't exactly the most profound sermon ever given and figuring the odds were against Skip Skip ever seeing it. But noticing the message could apply broadly, I copied and pasted it as a reply to several dozen other posters who seemed to need to read it for themselves. It was more likely that they would see it, and maybe one or two would actually take it to heart. Most of them would reply to my comment with something even more vulgar, maybe even threatening. But I'd never see it. I was done. I logged off and deleted the account entirely. So long, Skip Nation. See you never.

So many times we make the wrong choices but get an opportunity to change direction, I thought. Whether or not to palm the $10, then whether you place it in the barrel or in your pocket. Whether you head to the bar or to the rehab clinic after dropping off your kid. Whether you lash out in anger at someone or respond with silence or even kindness. And it feels like every right decision helps to train you for the next.

I heard it said that you can tell what your priorities are in life by looking at how you spend your time. It would be hard to add up all the hours I'd watched Skip Skip but I knew this time would be the last. But that would leave a hole in my weekly routine and it would be tempting to go back to him if I didn't come up with a better way to spend that time.

As I was about the turn off my phone and call it a night, an idea occurred to me to run one more internet search, and I typed "Christian social media."

15

It's Over

At the unexpected noise coming from the darkness of the living room as I staggered out of the bathroom, the thought did briefly occur to me that I was about to come across Santa Claus in action.

Just as quickly, though, I laughed at and dismissed the idea, chalking it up to still being half asleep. I hadn't looked at the time when I woke up early needing badly to relieve myself, weighing the pros and cons of just wetting myself before I reluctantly crawled out of bed, but as my now-emptied bladder and I went to investigate despite desperately wanting more sleep, I saw that the television was emitting more light than the windows were. It couldn't have been any later than about 6:00 a.m.

I made out a shadowy figure on one of the recliners just as I heard it ask, "Aren't you a little old to be waking up early on Christmas?"

"Hey Mom," I answered, recognizing the voice while my eyes were still adjusting. "I'm surprised you're not sleeping in yourself."

Of course, for Mom 'sleeping in' on weekends or holidays still meant that she'd be up around 7:00 a.m. Dad wouldn't wake for an hour or more after that. Even the girls slept like teenagers, my parents would joke, although on Christmas morning they'd likely be up sooner than later. They'd have to be, anyway, since we were going to church that morning before driving straight to my grandparents' house for a daylong visit with a big group of relatives on my mom's side of the family. My sisters were too old to participate in the pageant put on by the really little kids on Christmas Eve, but they both were members of the children's choir that would sing at 9:00 a.m. Mass.

"Just enjoying the peace and quiet," she answered, having found her happy place in her giant robe and slippers, a cup of coffee warming the hands she'd placed on her lap.

I grabbed a blanket at one end of the sofa and spilled myself across the cushions. "What are you watching?," I asked, too tired to walk back to my room and knowing myself well enough to sense that I wasn't likely to fall back asleep anyway.

"It's a replay of the Mass from the Vatican last night," she answered. I knew that took place at a church in Rome called St. Peter's Basilica and was celebrated by the Pope himself. Hundreds of people packed the church, with thousands more crowded outside together in an open area called St. Peter's Square.

"Cool, so if you and I watch this, we won't have to go to church today?" I asked. "I'll start opening my presents as soon as Dad leaves with the girls."

"Very funny," Mom said, knowing I knew better.

I watched and listened as a woman spoke at the pulpit in a language I didn't understand, while a pair of faceless announcers translated in English for the television viewers.

"That doesn't sound like Italian," I said.

"No, I'm guessing it's Portuguese," Mom answered. "They said she was from Brazil. This is the second reading. The first was read by a lady from the Philippines."

Despite the language barriers, the congregation all knew to stand as the second reading led to the singing of the "Alleluia." It reminded me of a time our family was vacationing far from home and attended Mass at a church that not only had a couple of minor different local customs, but a priest with a thick accent who we could barely hear from our seats in the back. Still, we were able to follow along since nearly everything else was so familiar. I told my dad then that it was the first time on that whole trip when I didn't feel like a stranger. "That's one of the beauties of belonging to the universal Church," he said. "You have family everywhere you go."

The television cameras panned along the congregation at St. Peter's as the Gospel concluded and the Pope prepared to deliver his homily.

"It's really beautiful, isn't it?" Mom commented before taking another sip of coffee.

"Yeah, it's a pretty awesome church," I replied.

"Sure, but I was thinking about everything going on around it," Mom said, pausing to put into words whatever it was that she was feeling. "All of those people from all over the world. Nobody cares whether they're more important than someone else, what country they're from, how much money they have, what they 'identify' as. They're there as brothers and sisters with their focus on God first and themselves last. And of course none of them are perfect but they know that, which is why they're there to begin with. Everyone else thinks they know the right way to build the perfect society...as long as you do it their way. And it always falls apart because everyone's idea means giving them control. Maybe we should try God's way. Maybe he has a better idea. He gave us the model for it, and we're looking at it right now."

Hearing the sound of approaching footsteps from the hallway, we both turned to see my dad enter the room in his typical bedtime outfit of an old tee shirt and shorts.

"Merry Christmas," he said sleepily. Noticing what was on television, he perked up and added, "Hey, good idea, let's just watch this instead of going to church."

He gave me a wink while Mom rolled her eyes and took another sip of coffee.

* * *

Dad pulled into the church parking lot a half hour before Mass since the girls needed to get there early with the rest of the choir. Even though the drive took just a few minutes, I couldn't wait to get out of the car after enduring my sisters' warm-ups, which consisted of them trying to outdo each other by seeing who could sing the highest notes possible. Somehow the car's windshield kept from shattering, but I wasn't sure I could say the same about my eardrums.

Despite our early arrival, the parking lot was already nearly full, with parishioners anticipating the need to secure their seats in what was always the most well-attended set of Masses of the entire year. As Dad pulled into a spot at least three times farther from the church than where we usually parked, I was prepared to hear his annual sarcastic commentary, which would usually go something like "Looks like everyone remembered they're Catholic and decided to finally haul their butts off to church so they could play dress-up and see the Baby Jesus. At least we won't have to worry about parking next week when they all go back into hibernation for another year."

To my surprise, he instead said, "Wow, what a huge turnout; that's great! Looks like you'll have a big audience, girls!" He turned to my mom who looked at him approvingly as they seemed to share one of those telepathic moments that only parents seemed to understand.

After my sisters scurried up to the choir loft, my parents and I walked past the back rows of pews that were packed with many unfamiliar faces – and several familiar faces I just hadn't seen for a while. We eventually located an empty space not far from where we normally sat in the middle of the church. As always before entering the pew, I genuflected to the tabernacle that holds the Blessed Sacrament, the consecrated hosts that have become the Body of Christ at a previous Mass. Kneeling next to my parents, I tried thinking of a prayer but found myself distracted by the decorations throughout the church. It really looked nice, with a large Christmas tree strung with simple white lights to one side of the altar, and a manger scene that was set up on the opposite side. Behind the altar as always was a large crucifix, a statue of Jesus nailed to the cross. I found myself looking back and forth between the images of that crucified man and the baby in the manger, knowing they were one and the same. Then the thought occurred to me that I could see him in a third place – the tabernacle. The difference was that he was really, truly, physically there, and in less than an hour, I would hold him in my hands and receive him. It was an awesome thought, if one took the time to really consider it. That baby in the manger, that man on the cross, the King of Kings. The most famous man in history, here in this place. God himself, the Creator of the Universe, was maybe 100 feet away from me, and soon to be within me.

It shouldn't have been a particularly original idea. It's something I've known as long as I can remember but it's all too easy to take it for granted as part of the routine of going to church every single week for years. For the first time in a long while, I was reminded of what the Mass is all about, and made a silent promise to reflect on that from now on, that even when all the emotion and excitement of Christmas wore off and life felt boring again, God is always here.

With several minutes still before the start of Mass, the children's choir began singing a few Christmas carols as the church continued to fill up to the point that even people who clearly weren't comfortable sitting in the front found themselves with no other options. I could make out Angela and Emily among the chorus of little voices, all of which sounded impressively melodic for a group of kids. I suppose I expected them all to instead be shouting over each other, but they were doing a nice job.

While the choir struck up its next song, I surveyed the pews ahead and across from me. Several rows up, I was surprised to see Tyler and his family in church for the first time in a long while. They were joined by a dark-haired girl who I took to be the girlfriend of one of Tyler's brothers. While his dad sat with his head down and his eyes closed, his mom rested her head on his shoulder, and I could see that they were holding hands.

The choir finished its last song, and as a man walked to the side podium to welcome everyone and direct them to the opening hymn in the songbook, four more people scurried up the aisle to find a seat. It was Nickie DeLorrio with her parents and daughter. As another family squeezed together to make space for them, I saw that Grace was carrying the stuffed unicorn, clutching it so tightly under one arm that I almost feared it would explode.

I guess she likes it, I thought to myself with a smile. Of course, it was really her mom that picked it out for her, and she'd know her own daughter's tastes. What I really should have wondered is what Nickie thought of the card I left for her in the gift bag a few nights earlier. While the unicorn was obviously meant for Grace, I scrawled Nickie's name on the outside envelope, and at the bottom of the card inside I had written:

Dear Nickie,

I'm sorry I didn't really answer your question about whether St. Mary's would be good for Grace. I think it's a great school that really helps all the students be good Christians. Sometimes some of us fail pretty miserably at that, as I suppose you know, but that's never the school's fault. They also teach you that when you do mess up, you take responsibility, learn from it, and do better the next time. I think I'd be a way bigger jerk if I didn't go there. I hope Grace likes the present.

Merry Christmas,

Jack

While I was surrounded in church by people mostly from my town, although surely there were visitors from elsewhere, I was thinking about the awe my mom expressed while watching the Mass from Rome that morning. We didn't come from all corners of the earth in this particular building in this particular town, but this same Mass at the same moment was taking place all over the world in thousands of churches and in hundreds of languages. In a cathedral in New York City and a tiny parish in rural Indiana. In both the urban Basilicas and village churches of Kenya and Mexico, in India and Ireland. In secret spaces in too many countries with garbage leaders that are too weak to allow their citizens to give glory to anyone but their idiot "rulers." And it happened not just on Christmas, not even just every Sunday, but every single day of the year. Every one of those hundreds of millions of people were truly connected to me, and I found it both overwhelming and comforting to think about being part of something so enormous.

Everyone at St. Mary's stood as the organist began playing the opening song, and I instinctively reached for a hymnal. While my parents considered lying to be the worst thing their kids could do, failing to sing in church was near the top of that list too, somewhere between getting bad grades and committing arson. Dad always said that he could tell the character of any boy under 18 who was humble enough to sing at church, or any man over 20 who was too proud to even read along and mouth the words. "I don't care about your husband's job or his favorite sports team," he once told my sisters, "but if you get engaged to a boy who can't be bothered to sing at Mass, don't bother inviting me to the wedding." I'm pretty sure he was just exaggerating to make a point. Plus, I didn't really believe the part about sports. There were some teams' fans whom he would absolutely struggle to accept into the family.

The altar servers and priest passed by our row, and I saw that Father Robert would be celebrating Mass. He must have asked Father Drew to handle the chaos of the children's Mass on Christmas Eve. I guess that's one of the benefits of being the pastor.

The liturgy started and proceeded as usual, with a few prayers and scripture readings unique to the occasion. After reading from the Gospel, Father Robert delivered his sermon, a portion of which stood out to me.

"Christmas is time for joy and peace," he said, "which we should carry in our hearts every day of the year, even amid our suffering. And there is suffering in this world, as there always has been. Today is Christmas...but the cross comes next. As soon as tomorrow we'll remember the first martyr, pummeled with rocks until he was killed because of his faith. Our faith. Soon after, we'll remember the Holy Innocents, children slaughtered by a jealous king desperate to hold onto his power. And that suffering is still with us today. Christians are still persecuted in many nations, and unborn children are allowed to be killed for votes and political power much closer to home.

"We don't like to think about those things today, not on Christmas. We want to adore the sweet little child, gaze in wonder at a sky filled with angels, place ourselves in the beauty and silence of the manger. We don't want to think about the child becoming a man who will be betrayed, tortured, and killed.

"But the manger and the cross go together and it's all a cause for our great joy! The final victory over sin and misery and death has been won. It's over. Understand that. It's over!

"It's trendy these days for people to say they want to be on 'the right side of history,' as if the value of their entire lives will be judged only by whether their political views at this tiny moment in human civilization will still be fashionable the day after they die. Oh, there is indeed a right side − be certain of that - but it's God's, not man's, and you had better be sure that you can tell the difference. Because the winning side and the losing side have already been determined! All that's left is for each of us to decide which side we'll join. But it's not 'us' against 'them' in this world. It's us against ourselves, and the choice is ours to make. Love God or ignore him. Follow Christ or abandon him. Love your neighbors or hate them.

"Yes, by all means, use this life to stand up for what's right, for the dignity of every one of God's creation. Do everything you can to make heaven on earth in your homes, your community, the world. But if we make enemies out of our fellow man - whether they're Catholics, atheists or anything in between - we make a choice to step closer to the losing side. It's not 'us' against 'them'. It's us against ourselves. The devil is still fighting battles over every one of us, but the war's already been won. By this little child. By Almighty God who became man out of love for you, to give you the freedom to have a chance at salvation and eternal life with him.

"What are you going to do with that freedom? Which choice are you going to make?"

Father Robert left those questions hanging in the air as he walked from the pulpit to his chair and carried on with the rest of the service. Half an hour later, the closing hymn was sung and most of the congregation began heading for the doors, stopping to chat with friends on their way out. My parents and I stayed in place to wait for my sisters.

"Good morning and Merry Christmas!" I heard a familiar voice say. "How are we on this blessed day?"

Mr. Leon had come over from wherever it was he'd been sitting to say hello to my parents and me. With him were his daughter, her husband, and three grandkids, apparently having traveled to spend Christmas with him. Two boys wore matching vests and bow ties over their shirts, while a little girl spun around in a green velvet dress. They looked as dashing as Mr. Leon always did, and while they waited politely, they clearly were itching to get on with the Christmas festivities at their grandpa's house.

As the adults continued talking, another recognizable voice got my attention.

"Merry Christmas, Jack!" said Nickie. Grace was at her side but was paying attention to her new toy. Nickie pointed at the unicorn and whispered, "Thank you."

"It's almost literally the least I could do," I said, still embarrassed that I'd put myself in the position of needing to do anything at all.

"No, the least you could have done was nothing," she replied. "And thanks for the note. It was perfect. Except the part about you being a jerk." I didn't bother arguing.

We left shortly after, and I climbed into the back of the car after letting my sisters in first. Mom tuned into a station playing Christmas carols as Dad started the engine for the drive to my grandparents'. The girls wasted no time in singing along and I turned to stare out the window so I could protect my ear closer to them from their noise. It would be even louder this afternoon with a couple dozen family members competing to make their voices heard, but I was looking forward to it.

We passed a car that looked like it was stuck in a small snowbank, but a couple was successfully pushing the back end out as the driver stepped on the gas and maneuvered into the open road, offering a wave of thanks as he drove on. The couple started walking back to their own car, parked nearby with two kids in the backseat. They surely had been on their way to go somewhere for Christmas, but made the decision to stop and help anyway.

Even before Father Robert's homily, I'd been thinking about how much power there is in the choices I make. Most of our decisions are little things that don't really matter, but even some of the big ones that would shape the rest of my life aren't all that important in the long run. Someday I'd have to decide whether to go to State U. or some other college, or skip it altogether. I might be a computer programmer or a mechanic or a store manager, and I could live in my hometown or move to a city. Those will be big, life-changing decisions but none of them matter if my priority is anything other than loving God first.

The choices that truly matter are the ones that line up with "*Follow Me,*" and even as an eighth grader I already knew most of what I needed to live that way. Spending time in prayer, knowing my faults and working on them, treating my family and friends and strangers with kindness. Even with things that are out of my control, I had the power to choose how to react. I didn't know what the future would bring, but even if something awful happened to me or to one of my parents, if the world seemed like it was falling apart around me, I'd still have the power to choose whether to love God or abandon him. Not only was it the only thing that truly mattered in my life, it was really the only thing under my control.

I think I can do that, I thought.

But you won't always want to, replied that voice in my conscience at the same time Angela accidentally elbowed me hard in the ribs as she gestured along to the music. That was true, I thought, resisting the urge to yell at my sister. It was easy to be forgiving and loving on Christmas Day, fresh out of church, but there'd be days I'd rather be in a crummy mood, or be more worried about what other people might think of me, or put my wants and needs ahead of others'. I guess those will be the times to put intellect and reason over feelings and emotions, doing what my mind *knows* is right even when my gut doesn't *feel* like doing the right thing.

I can do that, I thought, *with your help. Even though I'll screw it up a thousand times along the way, I can do that.* There was an overwhelming sense of freedom and comfort in knowing that as long as I put God first, there was absolutely nothing the world could throw at me that I couldn't handle.

As the car continued past rows of buildings adorned in colorful lights, I stared out the window with a feeling of peace and optimism and something else that I couldn't quite name until it came to me. I think the word for that is *hope*.

Made in the USA
Middletown, DE
06 January 2023